MW00944995

HIJACKED

into

PARADISE

How To Access Third Heaven And
Claim Your Potential

Dr. Wanda J. Sisco

www.xulonpress.com

DEDICATION

This book is dedicated to my Lord and Savior Jesus Christ! Thank You for inspiring me to dig deeper in my journey with You. Next, to my daughter, Jacqueline and my granddaughter, Ava; may the deposit of this book be something that will challenge you throughout your lives. You have inspired me to reach for greater and not settle for mediocrity! Finally to those who are not satisfied with the status quo of their spiritual lives, and to those who are seeking fulfillment from their spiritual walks. I challenge you to take full advantage of the full life of victory. Once you have read this book, get ready for a Third Heaven life!

TABLE OF CONTENTS

ACKNOWLEDGEMENTS

would like to acknowledge *The Daniel Initiative* and *Coles Creative Management* for their input and editing of this book. I also would like to thank all those who financially supported its publishing. Finally, to my sister, Daphne Tilly and the *Beyond the Veil* Intercessors for constantly interceding day and night for the success of this endeavor.

Third Heaven is perfect purity, and God wants to purify His saints on earth so they will enjoy heaven's atmosphere. Third Heaven is fullness of joy, and God desires to give joy to His people on earth. Third Heaven is everlasting freedom, and God longs for His people to have deliverance while on earth. Third Heaven is perfect wholeness, and God wants to heal His people here on earth. Third Heaven is complete security, and God wants His people to feel confident and secure here on earth. Third Heaven is fruition and fulfillment, and God desires that His people be fulfilled on earth. When Jesus instructed us to pray that God's will be done on earth as it is in heaven (Matthew 6:10), He revealed that God wants us to have a taste of Third Heaven here on earth!

PREFACE

In 2012, I began teaching a series on Third Heaven at my church. I was excited about the revelation that I was receiving from God. Sundays couldn't come soon enough, and I just knew that the members would be intrigued by these timely principles. After all, heaven is a subject that Christians frequently discuss. Sunday after Sunday I was pouring out my heart, preaching the message of Kingdom and of Third Heaven. And Sunday after Sunday my enthusiasm was matched with glazed over eyes, distant stares, and glares of just outright disinterest. Was I preaching the wrong message? Was I speaking another language? Maybe I had put too much stock in this revelation that I had just encountered, because not many people seemed to understand what I was saying.

It wasn't until about a year later that my congregation began to embrace parts of the message that I was teaching. Why did it take so long to even pique the interests of believers who had been "churched" for at least 12 years, and on such a "well-known" subject? I believe that it was primarily due to misconceptions and perceptions of heaven itself, and its reality. Man has a natural tendency to taint spiritual truths when we try to rationalize them from carnal perspectives. The subjects of heaven, angels, and eternal life are certainly no exception to this rule. I had spent an entire year demystifying heaven's realities, deconstructing preconceived notions, and replacing them with concrete biblical foundations. Sometimes I felt like the prophet Jeremiah who had to uproot and then plant again.

I also understood how Jesus felt when He began to teach about "eating His body and drinking His blood." When the disciples heard this, many of them said, "This is a hard and difficult and strange saying (an offensive and unbearable message). Who can stand to hear it?" [Who can be expected to listen to such teaching?] Many of His disciples drew back (returned to their old associations) and no longer accompanied Him. This had become the case with me, as well. However, those who dared embrace Third Heaven teaching began to have transformed lives, transformed prayers and their faith rose to new levels. Miracles began to happen as the demand for Third Heaven teaching began to resound from many different places. But before I could get to Third Heaven, I had to teach on the subject of heaven itself.

Over the last few years as a Pastor and a counselor, I have learned that the first step in introducing new teachings is to demystify or demolish mental barriers that already exist. There are countless examples of seed-stage revelations that are released improperly... "Delight yourself in the Lord, and He will give you the desire of your heart." How often has this scripture been used to make God an accomplice in our self-gratification and vain ambitions? We substantiate our claims by overstating how invested God is in our "happiness." In its proper context, this scripture is one of true submission to God's desires. For when you delight yourself in what God delights in, you in turn ask for what He desires for you. Then God gives you what you have asked, based on your expression of His desires in you. Preachers who will teach this truth to today's generation must first deconstruct the false perceptions that already exist. In the same way, our discussion on heaven has to set a tone that detaches it from prior notions. We should start with the fact that like the concept of paradise, heaven is a spiritual dimension that God intended for man to enjoy here on earth first.

INTRODUCTION

*"You've forced me to talk this way, and I do it against my better judgment. But now that we're at it, I may as well bring up the matter of visions and revelations that God gave me. For instance, I know a man who, fourteen years ago, was seized by Christ and swept in ecstasy to the heights of heaven. I really don't know if this took place in the body or out of it; only God knows. I also know that this man was **hijacked into paradise…"** [2 Corinthians 12:1-4 Message Bible]*

Encounters are good. Every encounter has its place. But for most of us, once the encounter is over, it becomes a blur. The instant the encounter happens, we receive a vision or revelation that we say will forever change our lives! But once the ecstasy and excitement have subsided, we tend to return to our mundane lives in a place called complacency. That is until we have a *self-encounter*. It is a place where you come face-to-face with who you are now and who you can potentially become. At this place, you see wonderful possibilities and wonder how to bridge the gap between what you see now; and how to get where you see yourself in the future. Some choose to embrace this new place, while the vast majority decide to walk away empty-handed and unfulfilled. Some think: "Is this all there is to life? Is this as good as it gets?" I encourage you to challenge your limits. Get everything God has for you without leaving earth. Move from mediocrity to exceptionality! The graves are filled with unclaimed potential.

This gap can cause frustration through unanswered or obstructed prayers. We know that prayer is important. As children, we are taught the value of the most simplistic prayers. Movies depict prayer from the youngest to the oldest; from every nation, creed and color. Prayer is not an unusual phenomenon. However, for many, this has become a place of unspoken desperation – a place where you feel as though you have hit a brick wall. And for most of us, at times, it's hard to follow God's lead…unsure of what He wants us to do. You may feel that you have done everything that you know to do. You have aligned and positioned yourself to be able to effectively navigate through to the next level, but to no avail. The problem with levels is: they are managed systems that we feel we can maneuver our way through. For instance, once we finish and master the third grade level, the next level is the fourth grade. Could it be that we need to think in terms of dimensions instead of levels? Dimensions are normally out of our control, but once we learn that they exist and are places where God controls every aspect of our progress; then we can effectively operate with Him in order to make effective progress through life. For instance, months or maybe even years may have passed with little or no progress in a particular area of your life. Could it be that your prayers have never left the realm of what is seen? After all, don't we pray to a God Who is not seen? Although God may not appear to us in a vision or a dream, He makes Himself known to us in many ways….after all He is the Creator of the universe around us as well as the universe inside of us. And yes, there is a universe inside of us orbiting around its core called "self."

It is the intent of the author that the Holy Spirit will use this book to free those who seem trapped in a dimension where their prayers are heard, yet unanswered. Those whose cries for help seem to have gone unanswered (and a sense of unbelief has taken over) are about to discover the keys to accessing and maintaining open heavens. The Bible has much to say about the spirit realm where our lives are concerned.

This book is a response to the cries of Christians' frustration to routine, mundane, practical and careful teaching tools through which we shall know more about the heavens, heavenly places, where they are located, where we are located in relation to them, and our authority concerning them. It takes a close look at how we can powerfully move through the First, Second and Third Heavens causing change in the believer's total life. I am therefore dedicated to making this book useful to the believer. Knowledge is indeed power!

My intention is not to try to satisfy the defiant appetites of the ever-present skeptics who will always remain insatiably hungry for criticism, nor is it to feed a name-it claim-it way of misguided living a pie-in-the sky lifestyle. I pledge not to become fixated upon opinion, but instead to focus on the apostolic teaching of how God works through dimensions to fulfill the mission of heaven here on earth using men and women who truly have an understanding of Kingdom principles and perspectives.

The answer to your dilemma might be just as simple as determining "What heaven you are operating in!"

CHAPTER 1
PARADISE LOST

*P*aradise! The very word invokes thoughts of serenity, peace, limitless amounts of happiness, and pleasure that can't be adequately expressed with other words. It is a concept that many advertisers and salesmen capitalize on. Though paradise and heaven are often seen as synonymous in concept, it is interesting to note that books on paradise slightly outnumber books on heaven. This may possibly be due to the fact that the concept of heaven is predominately embraced by religious sects, while paradise is universally accepted as an end-state. The voluminous amount of content on this subject can credit its popularity to the high demand for, and inquisitive nature of paradise. People chase after money, jockey for better employment, and seek to climb up the social ladder out of the desire to achieve this end-state called paradise. It has become a mundane ideal that is posited as the end-result of a lifetime of hard work, achievement, and effort, not unlike the notion of the "American Dream." So what exactly is paradise? What is this paradise that Paul refers to when he claims that he had met someone who was caught up into paradise? Whether it's an actual physical place or a state of mind depends on whom you ask. For some "paradise" is a better job; for others it is defined as more peace. There are still others who take the traditional view of paradise as heaven, where there is no sickness, dying, and all needs are met. Paradise has essentially become defined in subjective terms as a better alternative to what we consider to be currently inadequate in our lives. However, in order to fully understand the concept of paradise, we should consider its creator, origin, and intent. In essence, we must first define the laws of creation to ensure that we have the proper understanding of paradise. Does paradise really exist? And if it is real, how and when can we experience it?

"In the beginning, God created the heavens and the earth"... this familiar passage from Genesis is the nexus to all that we know and understand of creation. Paul would later corroborate this by describing the "unknown God" to the Athenians as "the God that made the world and all things therein, seeing that he is Lord of heaven and earth." So it was God who created everything that we are able to sense, see, and have. God saw a formless earth and began to bring order to the chaos. In essence God manifested all that we see pertaining to the heavens and the earth. All of these things originated with Him and are under His control. God Himself is the only One who can create things in the sense of origins. We must then believe that God "is," and that earth was not some random chaotic experiment, but the calculated and strategic brain thrust of God. With this creationist foundation, there are laws of creation that are important to our understanding paradise.

"The Will to Exist"

Many scientists define the first law of creation as "I wish to exist." The basic frame of their understanding is one of humanism, a framework that attributes more power to the creatures and creations more than their creator. Yes, it is true that "as a man thinketh in his heart, so is he," yet this is not speaking of original creative acts, but rather sustained acts. No earthly or celestial being possesses the intellect or independent will to exist from nothing. That power is reserved for God alone, Who has no traceable origin or start date. Therefore, the first law of creation is that there must be present *"the will to exist."* God alone had that will to exist that He carried for the heavens, earth, entire universe, and everything therein. This law is perfectly fitting when ascribed to God. When God created the heavens and the earth, it literally existed because He *willed* it to be so. Out of His sheer Will, this great God made the thoughts of His Mind manifest into actual reality! What an amazing concept! Think of the idea that God created the heavens, the earth, and the universe out of the thoughts of His Mind. He alone carried the will for humanity and all of creation to *be*, and from the beginning of our very existence the destiny of the entire world would be tied to God alone. To deny His existence would be to deny our reality.

"The Will to Function"

If creation is a product of God's thoughts, then this suggests that He made it with an intent and plan. It is impossible to detach manifested thoughts from their intentions. God did not haphazardly think of the earth, the heavens, the animals, or humanity without a strategic functionality for each of them. In essence, He not only had an intention for us to exist, but also a will for us to function. These functions work concertedly within the confines of God's masterful purpose. Genesis tells us that God made man "in His image and likeness," and then expresses His intended functionality for them in the earth: *"and let them have dominion over the fish of the sea, and over the fowl of the air, and over the cattle, and over all the earth, and over every creeping thing that creepeth upon the earth."* That man was meant to have dominion comes from the will that God placed within him to also function in accordance with God's overall purpose. Man was made to function, to "do something." Everyone's "something" may be different, but we all share an inner drive, innately given by our Creator to carry out a work on earth. The most frustrating aspect of unemployment is not the financial handicap, but the helpless inability to function as one believes they are sanctioned. God willed for man to exist, and then gave man the will to want to function according to specific purpose. There is an explicit work for each person to perform, and it is natural to feel a unique burden to fulfill this function in alignment with destiny. What is at work is the law of the will to function.

"The Law of Partnerships"

God stamps the seal of His image and powerful likeness on man, and then commands man to operate out of this reality. God did not simply command man, but rather placed His own power within man as a necessary resource to fulfill His purpose. Man, endowed like God, was meant to be the ambassador and representative of this Divine entity on the earth. In essence, God enters a partnership with man to bring and maintain God's purpose and Kingdom from heaven to earth. This partnership was a great amount of trust and responsibility that was freely given by God to man. Yet this strong bond was also fragile, built on the single strand of man's willingness to remain in complete alignment and obedience to the original intent of God's creation. **The law of partnerships is as follows: shared responsibility properly upheld ensures shared success.** Think of partnerships in the business sense. They are based on the trust that both parties hold for one another, as well as their commitment to the integrity of their original shared philosophy. Business mergers, marriages, and friendships: in each case the success of these relationships depends on the strength of the partnerships. Paul in his second letter to Timothy acknowledges this law when he declared: *"It is a faithful saying: for if we be dead with him, we shall also live with him: If we suffer, we shall also reign with him."* God could have reigned sovereignly alone without the cognizance of man, making us mere robots doing His bidding. However, God saw the long-term value in partnering with man. Partnerships produce long-term relationships that can help propel ideals to a majority of society. It also gave man the ability to not only steward earth's destiny with God, but to also share in the successful reigning with God. He had afforded man this paradise, and it was His intent to spread that benefit amongst Adam and all his future descendants. From the very beginning, God made room for man to exist, function, rule, and then reap the shared benefits of that dominion. The greatest sign of true kingdom success is the ability of the monarch to empower and share both responsibility and wealth with his or her citizens. Kingdoms where wealth is grossly unbalanced result in the eventual destruction of those societies. If wealth is highly concentrated within the monarchy, yet heavily lacking amongst the citizens, the dissatisfaction amongst the people either empower them to depose the elite power, or become a vulnerable prey to repressive dictatorships. Alternately, systems where wealth and power are concentrated amongst the general population at the expense of an underdeveloped leadership imperil the ability of the monarch to lead. God in His infinite wisdom decided that the best way to ensure that paradise could be enjoyed by humanity was through the law of partnerships.

"The Law of Fulfillment"

God willed for us to exist, and out of that will assigned the functionality of dominion. As long as man was completing his God-ordained purpose, all that he needed was readily taken care of by God. **The law of fulfillment proposes that maintaining**

proper balance and equilibrium with God's Will automatically provide fulfillment and satisfaction for everything that is necessary for life both spiritually and physically. When Adam was working the Garden and in constant fellowship with God, he experienced fulfillment. Eden was a garden that was rich with minerals and natural resources. It was abundant in gold, bdellium, and onyx stones, with water in great supply. As Adam worked the Garden, in submission to God's system, all that he needed was within reach. The earth also experienced fulfillment with a constant mist rising from the ground ensuring that the earth was immediately quenched of its thirst. With all of the resources just a stroke away, Adam was not working this work out of necessity for survival. He was not living from paycheck to paycheck, nor "making ends meet." He was working out of a worshipful and obedient love for the God Who had partnered with his dusty frame and given him dominion and purpose. He was never more fulfilled in life than when he was working within the proper guise and alignment that God had foreordained. This may be why Jesus adequately stated *"my meat is to do the will of Him that sent me."* Even for Jesus, obedient love and submission to the Father was His sustenance and fulfillment. He had no greater pleasure than to be in proper alignment with God, and out of that flowed all the peace, joy, and satisfaction that He needed.

Somehow, within the few verses that are allotted to it, Eden has lost its true allure in today's context. Eden was a beautiful place that defied comparisons or parallels. There was not another place that was as peaceful and pleasant as Eden. Yet the nexus of all this alluring beauty was the Presence of God that walked with Adam and Eve in the "cool of the day." That was heaven on earth with everything from the physical aspects to the spiritual and conceptual benefits that man enjoyed. In this model all the physical needs that man had were met, and every aspiration and desire fulfilled. Adam and Eve enjoyed limitless joy, peace, prosperity, security, and freedom. Mankind possessed paradise. Paradise was physical, spiritual, and conceptual; it is all of these things, and could only be accessed through the proper equilibrium that was alignment with God. It was this fragile bond that was earth's proudest moment; yet the severing of this bond brought earth to its most chaotic state from which it still presently suffers.

When was this great reality of paradise lost? It is interesting to note that Satan, or evil, as we know it, existed during this time of the earth's golden renaissance. His existence on earth predated the creation of man, as his origin was actually with God in the beginning. Yet amidst his presence in the earth, due to his fall, man still enjoyed a close bond with God and partnership with this King of all things. So the loss of paradise was not due to the presence of evil. Paradise, and all of its benefits were lost when man chose to align with another system outside of the Will and intent of what God had deemed appropriate. The eviction of paradise's full experience on earth was due to Adam's errant rebellious choice against God's Kingdom directives. *"The day you eat of the fruit of the tree of the knowledge of good and evil, you shall surely die."* These words by God were the promise not of instant physical death, but the death of spiritual separation and connection with His Voice. Though the object of the serpent's temptation to man was fruit; an alternate system was what was actually being sold. I can imagine the subtle serpent with a passive look as he offered Eve this seemingly delectable and appealing fruit. Though his outward manner seemed to be blasé, he understood that what stood on the other side of this choice was the disruption of man's peaceful life as they knew it. Their choice for this new system was simultaneously a rejection of God's perfect spiritual ecology. With Adam and Eve's fall came the collapse of all the peace, joy, provision, and fulfillment that man naturally experienced. All of these necessities were experienced effortlessly under God, yet part of man's punishment was henceforth to laboriously slave for things once labeled unbridled rights. The earth, once easily tamed by man's natural authority, now had to be closely managed and subdued. Therefore, the very ideal of paradise moved from a reality to a conceptual theory when man rejected his proper alignment under God. It is very easy for us to demonize Adam for his shortsightedness; however, how much power and authority have we willingly given up due to our short-term personal ambitions? How often have we as believers forsaken the right to paradise for a slice of temporary satisfaction? Paradise was lost at Adam and Eve's fall, yet it also continues to be forfeited by major blocks of the Church on a daily basis. When we choose to shut out God's ability to reign freely in our lives, we lose paradise. The loss of His complete Presence, the nearness of His Voice, His willing rule in our lives turns our ideal paradise into a world of ruins. Money, peace, happiness, and complete health; these aspects alone are not paradise. Yet when we are properly aligned under God's system in obedient love, these "things" become the by-product of true paradise: fellowship with God. There is a line of a well-known hymn, written by Charles Converse, that is befitting of the root of the world's societal ails: *"O what peace we often forfeit, O what needless pain we bear, all because we do not carry everything to God in prayer."* How much longer will we continue to labor for life's God-given promises because we neglect to align properly under God's system? Paradise was once lost, but the purpose of this book is to remind you that it has been restored and can be experienced in your lifetime! However, before paradise can be regained, we must figure out what personal hindrances have kept us from experiencing the fullness of this manifestation. The following questions are meant to help you as you identify potential obstacles to your growth.

QUESTIONS:

- How have I defined paradise and its accessibility to me?

- What areas of my life are properly aligned under God's system?

- What areas of my life seem to be out of alignment with God's vision of paradise for me?

CHAPTER 2
PARADISE REGAINED

aradise was lost when Adam and Eve exchanged their intimate constant connection with God for a system of self-provision and self-gratification. The Presence of our creative Deity was the fulfillment of every true need that we would experience; yet in one fell swoop the partnership was broken as we decided to "go it alone." The funny thing is that for all the grandeur of this system that seemed good in one moment of temptation, the reality was actually a chaotic world of perpetual delusions. Adam's fall led to Cain offering improper sacrifices to God, yet thinking it was comparable to what God actually required. The Tower of Babel saga was another poor attempt to "go it alone"; trying to accomplish great feats with the tools that God gave man, all the while absent and separate from the

Creator Himself. Vain imaginations became the order of the day, as we would craft shrines and creations that were odes to our self-importance and entitlements. Even many churches today put God's Name on many spiritual and physical structures that are really only pathways for more self-emulation. Yes, this was the inherent cycle that we had bought as part of our fall. It is a world where we would errantly attribute the works of God's Hands to our own human intellect and capability. This false narrative would be passed down from generation to generation until the true meaning of paradise slowly faded from our conscience. Paradise was now a code word for a "fulfilled self" as determined by the creations and not by the standards of a Creator. Paradise was no longer a nearness to God where the very heavens of His residence permeated the earth. It had soon become a mirage, where the best that we could hope for was cars, houses, more money than we could dream, and the list goes on. We were in breach of our partnership agreement, yet we chose to continue under a "business as usual" assumption.

We should probably pause here to contemplate the realities of God's choice at this point. He could have decided that we were forever a product of our own choices and given us over to the endless cycles of delusion and failure. He could have continued reigning as the sole successful partner in this breached agreement and collect the benefits all to Himself. Surely any sane businessman would never allow himself to be burned or taken at a disadvantage. Our actions have legal ramifications, of which the suitable punishment is certain and unrelenting spiritual death. However, God chose none of these "First Heaven responses." One of the many qualities that makes Him God is His steady resolve to operate out of Who He is, and not out of how He feels. In the midst of all His options, God decided that He would still prefer to live up to the original partnership agreement that He had initiated and set forth. This pathway meant that paradise is still a possibility for man to attain, however it could not be accessed without properly returning to the tenants of realignment under God. The mercy of our God is to still leave the original offer on the table. While we remain busy trying to "go it alone," God constantly strives to succeed by including man in this excellent promise of paradise. It doesn't seem like a fitting or just reward for a world that sold itself to selfish endeavors, yet this is what makes Him stand alone as God.

Yes paradise was still an option for humanity, but something was needed to rescue us from the fruitless cycle that we had produced. First through Moses, the law was instituted as a system to reinstitute God's laws for us. However, this was not enough, as *"it was impossible for the blood of bulls and goats to take away sins."* [Hebrews 10:4, KJV] These sacrifices were symbolic gestures at best that could not reach to the core of our issue: the inner man. The fall was a violation of God's laws that were the product of choice, or a warped mindset. The only thing that could break the cycle of improper thought, or free us from spiritual paralysis was a spiritual substitute wrapped in a fleshly garment. In other words we were in need of God Himself coming in the flesh through Jesus Christ.

Our faith in Christ as our sacrifice was not to merely save us from our sins. He did not come from heaven solely to staunch the cycle of sins, but to really reconnect us in fellowship with God the Father. What is the difference, and does it matter? The answer is emphatically, yes! It does matter! The difference is that man could attempt to live as we have deemed "sinless" and still miss the mark because we would be no closer to a genuine connection with God. During His intercessory prayer,

Jesus states that His mission was to bring eternal life to those who God had given to Him [John 17:2 KJV]. He then defines eternal life in relational terms: *"that they might **know** thee the only true God, and Jesus Christ whom thou hast sent." [John 17:3 KJV]* The Greek term *ginosko* denotes a personal and intimate knowledge. This type of knowledge cannot be attained by reading books or transmitted by proxy through someone else's account. This ability to *know* can only be gained by personal experience. God can only be encountered on an intimate level through Christ. Essentially God was using Christ as the vehicle to restore man to the original schematic of paradise, which was a nearness to God in thought, proximity, and action. To put it another way, Christ was God's plan for us to regain paradise.

Sometimes we glorify Christ's death at the expense of missing the lessons that His life taught us. Too often we become cheerleaders in the stands, when we were meant to join Him on the field of victory. How was it that Jesus would empower us to regain paradise? It would be by refocusing our thoughts and spirit man to God's original partnership agreement from the days of Eden. He admonished the people of His time to set aside their own system of providing for themselves, and forsake the original tradeoff that landed man into their delusional cycle. Rather they should again submit to God's plan by seeking first His Kingdom, and its way of living. In other words man should repent, recalibrate, and realign.

Repent

From the beginning man was given free will, and it was God's greatest crowning achievement in His creation of them. He wanted man's worship, adoration, and affection, but He wanted it *willingly*. This great asset of man ended up being the downfall of man. Though the serpent was subtle, man chose to forsake God's way. The fall was not a result of an uncontrollable possession from which man needed an exorcism, but the product of errant choice. Therefore, the flaw was not in the devil's cunning argument, but in the wandering mind of humanity. This is why John the Baptist and Jesus repeated one word as the opening line of their mass appeal: REPENT!!! It is such an important word, and simultaneously quite misunderstood in contemporary times. Many Christians confuse repentance and sorrow, when the two are significantly different. Sorrow is an emotional state while repentance is a mental shift. Have you ever heard the saying "godly sorrow leads to repentance?" This principle, found in 2 Corinthians 7:10, classifies sorrow and repentance as two separate yet related entities, but never to be confused as synonymous. It is possible to be sorry about something while continuing to enact the same egregious offenses. I can recall numerous instances where I've heard someone apologize to me, only to forge ahead with acts of injustice and betrayal. This is because sorrow is a feeling that people experience, like guilt. However, this feeling alone is not enough to change behavioral patterns. Repentance however, is a horse of a different color. It is a psychological state or mentality change. Offenders with no remorse are dangerous, and people who feel sorry but neglect to see the error of their ways present similar hazards. Renowned atheist George Santayana is attributed with expressing sentiments that led to the quote "those who do not learn from history are doomed to repeat it." While his religious philosophies differ widely from the Christian worldview, Santayana posited a valid point. Those who are sorry but do not assess where they erred end up repeating the same mistakes, and are unable to repent. Repentance means to rethink, assess, and turn around in one's mindset. What John the Baptist and Jesus were advocating for in their "three-step" sales-pitch was to first consider the mental flaws that incarcerated man, and perpetuated our failures. Just as clearly as we choose the system of sin and selfishness, we would be required to choose to reject that system in support of God's Kingdom. Paradise was ended due to a mind shift, and it could be regained through a return to the original mentality.

Just think back to every regret that you have had; the seed of that mistake was an errant thought. No amount of sorrow could undo the damage that you may have caused. The only fitting remedy was a change in your way of thinking. A thought that acknowledged your way as evil; and then an alternate thought that recognized God's way as the best pathway.

Recalibrate

The entirety of Christ's message was "repent for the kingdom of heaven is at hand." The first part of that message, repent, called for a mental shift. The second half of the message was a call to action that had two parts: recalibrate, and realign. After all "… the Kingdom of God is not in word, but in power."[1 Corinthians 4:20 KJV] Power is an active term and an action word. Power is denoted by its visibility, its success, and not its intentions. Once the mindset has been changed due to repentance, it must then express this repentance through changed actions. As Paul eloquently stated, we should not conform, but instead be transformed by a renewed mind. Transformation is an inward change that is reflected outwardly for all to see. Recalibration is the process of measuring again to ensure the accuracy of an instrument. After repentance, we must then look at life, kingdom, and paradise through this different lens to assess what new actions are necessary in accordance with the observed reality. A repentant mind can readily acknowledge the need for Jesus Christ as Lord and Savior, and then is ready to rely on the Holy Spirit to recalibrate. Why? Because the Spirit knows the Mind of God, and thus is the most accurate measure of the appropriate actions needed to effectively operate in paradise.

One major benefit to recalibration is that it increases the potential longevity of the instrument. Worrying about First Heaven issues like clothes, food, shelter, and employment are short-term distractions that derail the ability of believers to abide in the truth of Third Heaven reality of fulfillment. However, recalibrating the mind to prioritize Kingdom as the primary pursuit gives believers access to enduring tools suitable to attain paradise here on earth.

Realign

Wise movements are based upon calculated premises. The beautiful reality of John's three-point message was that it was predicated on the calculated premise that: (1) repentance could be attained through Jesus Christ; (2) a new outlook, or recalibration was accessible through the Holy Spirit; and thus (3) realignments, or wise movements, provide repositioning to regain paradise. Realignment is the process of putting things back in their proper order. In fact this definition is suitable for the process many Christians experience post salvation. For the believer, this life is all about putting things back into their proper prioritized places based on our new outlook in Christ. When we are properly realigned under God's divine order, paradise is then accessible to us.

Paradise was lost to us through the fall of Adam. We must realize however, that paradise was regained by Jesus Christ who bridged the gap for all who would believe. It is true that you can have your best life now. Heaven was meant to be brought to earth and not only experienced post-mortem. The message of Christ in regaining paradise was through repentance, recalibration, and realignment, and this message still holds true to this very day. You don't have to wait another day to experience your paradise regained, because it was always God's design to open this reality up to you. Why wait? Experience your new day today by asking yourself the following questions:

- **What areas of my life or thought process are in need of repentance?**
- **What areas of my life must be recalibrated to God's measure of effectiveness?**
- **Are my actions of realignment stemming from a repentant heart and recalibrated mind?**

The intent of the author is that every reader gets to experience the full revelation of Third Heaven and its accessibility on earth. Based on the fact that Christ is the only way to true salvation and eternal life, it is imperative that Jesus Christ be offered to every reader. If you are unsaved, but wish to accept Christ as your Lord and Savior pray the prayer of Faith provided below:

> *Jesus I confess that I am a sinner in need of Your grace and mercy. I repent of my sins. I denounce my trust in the works of darkness, and I confess that Jesus Christ died on the cross for my sins. I believe that God raised Jesus Christ from the dead, and that through Christ I now have access to God the Father. I accept Jesus Christ as my Savior and Lord of my life, and from this day on I am saved!*

If you prayed this prayer, I am excited to welcome you to the Body of Christ, and to the first day of your ability to access heaven on earth! As you continue to grow in your new life in Christ, I pray that the rest of this book gives you the tools you need to live in the reality of paradise that God has foreordained for you to enjoy in this present day!

CHAPTER 3
THE HEAVENS

*"First, this: God created the Heavens and the
Earth — all you see, all you don't see." [Genesis
1:1 Message Bible]*

ost people bristle with curiosity and excitement
at the mention of the place called heaven. What
will it be like? Where is it exactly? Who is able to get there?
How will it feel to be in a place of pure serenity, no stress, no
sickness, or pain? Immense pleasure and joy mixed with the
sweet fragrance of God's nearness. Images of huge locked iron
gates (with an angelic security detail at the helm) fill our minds.
Or perhaps we envision God sitting at the front gate with His
sharpened quill pen ready to check the books for the names of

those who RSVP'd ahead of time. We often think of heaven in abstract terms, as if it is some far away world that we can only experience in the "sweet by and by." The Bible is full of details about heaven. God describes heaven as His throne, or place of authority. John describes a sea of glass with the four and twenty elders bowing in submission at the throne. Daniel describes an encounter with the Archangel Gabriel, who had been detained temporarily in the heavens by the Prince of Persia. It is as if God has strategically revealed choice and select morsels of these mysterious heavens, so that we could desire this unseen realistic entity.

It sometimes feels cruel that a place with such prominent future implications seems just shy of our human reach, yet near enough to flood our hearts and thoughts. We live our lives, choose relationships, subscribe to religious doctrines, and even sow financially off of this notion of some other world that we will experience after death. I certainly do not wish to suggest that these notions aren't factual, but rather expose the latent mentality that we can only experience heaven later instead of sooner. Heaven is far more than an adjective or an attitude. It is a reality, the reality of every believer, our reality to grasp. This place called heaven is our "now" moment, and it was meant to be experienced on earth. This is why Christ would teach us to pray "thy Kingdom come, thy will be done on earth as it [*already*] is in heaven." He was teaching us how to make room for heaven to invade earth. Unfortunately today, many Christians are living life with both eyes on the exit sign, instead of upholding our end of the partnership agreement ratified by God in the beginning.

"Rediscovering Heaven On Earth"

You are a spiritual being; yes you, reading this book. Wrapped in flesh, you are a spiritual being that inhabits this earth. I know it seems like a crazy ideal, but your flesh is just the shell casing that is animated by the real you, the life force, your spirit. We often quote Genesis when we say that we were made in God's image and likeness. We also often mistake this to mean that God's image is referring to our outward appearance. God doesn't look like us physically. He doesn't have tan skin, blue eyes, white pearly teeth, or a receding hairline. God is a Spirit. He is the invisible and unseen God. When God formed man He was creating a being with a spiritual nexus. Everything was meant to emanate and revolve around this spiritual inner man. Your thoughts, desires, and actions were always meant to flow from the real you. In fact, when people speak of others giving off "bad vibes"; they are referring to something spiritual. Life was meant to be viewed and experienced from a spiritual perspective. I don't mean this in the spooky sense, being so spiritually-minded that we forget to function here on earth. We must take the necessary steps to ensure that we are nourishing our physical body, so that we can exist in this earth. However, our primary outlook should be to live life primarily on a spiritual plane, understanding that the decisions we make from this place eventually affect our physical state. Your most delightful quality is not your physical makeup, your smile, or your "charming" personality; it is your spirit man. It is this part that was made and crafted in the exact image of God. In fact, due to our makeup, our true desires are actually spiritual in nature instead of natural. Think about it. We believe that what we desire for fulfillment are houses, cars, land, or money. However, there are plenty of rich people seeking happiness, landowners lacking joy, and Cadillac owners bereft of peace. We spend a lifetime pursuing material things like this, and are never truly satisfied even when we do achieve the end of "the chase." The reality is that we desire spiritual fulfillment, even though we ascribe those yearnings to natural pursuits. Why? The answer is because we are spiritual beings that desire spiritual things. Philippians 4:19 states *"But my God shall supply all your need according to his riches in glory by Christ Jesus."* This scripture indicates that there is one need that when fulfilled completes us. That need is a relationship with God through Jesus Christ. It's spiritual!

God made the proto-type Adam in His image, *tselem*. In its Hebrew connotation, this word distinctly means a representative figure. Adam was not unlike a Kingdom Ambassador, sent to an earthly Embassy to represent God in the earth. No matter how far away an Ambassador is from the homeland, his/her embassy resembles the atmosphere and customs of the home territory. An American Ambassador in Turkey will still have a U.S. flag on the premises. He or she will eat traditional American foods, and listen to their favorite music from home. They would also keep in close contact with the American government. Part of these actions is maintained out of a need to personally experience a continual interaction with the culture that developed them. However, the purpose of the Embassy and the Ambassador is to influence the surrounding foreign culture with the American culture. Its dynamic purpose is to promote American culture, or bring America to Turkey. Likewise, Adam was a Kingdom Ambassador meant to bring the heavenly realm or culture to the earthly realm or culture. We, as God's representatives, are meant to bring the culture of heaven to earth. This means bringing God's dictates, customs, way of thinking, and way of living to earth. It is the Matthew 6:33 principle at work that Jesus introduced to society. The heaven(s), created in the beginning by God, were always meant to be experienced by humanity as part of our earthly mandate.

In 2 Corinthians 12:2-11, the Apostle Paul was *"seized by Christ and swept in ecstasy to the heights of heaven."* In order to understand the place that Paul describes we must first have a correct understanding of where he initially was. Some translations of the Bible refer to this paradise as Third Heaven, or the highest heaven. This eternal residence was a surreal dimension full of unmentionable happenings and unfathomable experiences. This was no ordinary earthly encounter; nothing Paul could compare it to. Have you ever experienced something so extraordinary that you had nothing to measure it by? The type of occurrence that you couldn't adequately explain even if you tried…and when you try to express it, you find that most of the people around you aren't able to handle the revelation that you've received. These are the feelings that Paul faced after interacting with paradise. He had heard Jesus' teachings on the kingdom of heaven, like everybody else. Heaven was an elusive concept, a faraway promise to the Jews and the believing Gentiles of that day. Jesus had described what the kingdom of heaven was like, including its rules, customs, and norms. Yet this Apostle, who hadn't even experienced Jesus' earthly ministry firsthand, is selected to enjoy the reality of His teachings. What Paul had experienced was not just heaven, but Third Heaven. It stands to reason therefore, that if Third Heaven exists, then there is also a First and Second Heaven. So what exactly is the concept of Heaven?

Scripture generally speaks of heaven as the abode of God. Moses prayed that God would *"look down from your holy house in Heaven"* (Deuteronomy 26:15). Jesus prayed to *"Our Father in heaven"* (Matthew 6:9). It is a key mark of Christian confession that God created not only the earth, but also the full extent of the heavens.

Heaven is the circumference of things created, both visible and invisible. Contained within its boundary are the mental faculties of the angels and all the world of sense. When God made the heavens and the earth, His creative employ was not random but strategic and orderly. God made the heavens and all therein in a systematic manner, making certain things before others. The first things created were the empyrean heavens (the place in the highest heaven – dwelling place of God, source of light and creation); formless corporeal matter (e.g., angels); and time (both chronos and kairos) – all these things fashioned on the first day.

Genesis 1:1 "First this: God created the Heavens and the Earth – – all you see, and all you don't see." [Message Bible]

Hebrews 11:3 "By faith we understand that the worlds [during the successive ages] were framed (fashioned, put in order, and equipped for their

*intended purpose) by the word of God, so that
what we see was not made out of things which are
visible)." [Amplified Bible]*

During the six days of the Genesis regeneration the Lord defined Three Heavens. First Heaven is the Earth's atmosphere where men and women dwell.

Second Heaven is the vast expanse of the physical universe – outer space as we call it. According to Ezekiel 8:3, it is between the earth and the heavens. It is where the seat of the idol (image) of jealousy dwells. It is the place of warfare or the place where war is waged for power over First Heaven (the earthly realm).

Third Heaven is above Second Heaven. Ephesians 2:6 states, *"And He raised us up together with Him and made us sit down together (giving us joint seating with Him) in the heavenly sphere (by virtue of our being) in Christ Jesus (the Messiah, the Anointed One)."*

Undoubtedly when most Christians speak of heaven, it is in eschatological terms, referring to the end times. Simply put, we believe that the present world will vanish away, and there will be "a new heaven and a new earth" (Isaiah 65:17; 66:22).

Without a sense of terror or anxiety, the psalmist expected that ultimately all things (including the heavens) would pass away, yet life with God would not end: "*Long ago thou didst lay the foundation of the earth, and the heavens were thy handiwork. They shall pass away, but thou endures; like clothes they shall all grow old; thou shalt cast them off like a cloak, and they shall vanish; but thou art the same and thy years shall have no end; thy servants' children shall continue, and their posterity shall be established in thy presence*" (Psalm 102:25-28).

The heavens are a reality, and as Paul's experience conveys, Third Heaven does exist. The Apostle experienced this dimension while he was alive and breathing, which means heaven was always meant to be accessed while here on earth. Heaven is not only a dimension or realm, but is essentially where God dwells and He rules. Accessing heaven is actually about capturing God's heart and allowing Him to dwell with us. To experience life from His viewpoint and reality is heaven on earth.

QUESTIONS:

- **What do you believe about heaven? (Whatever you believe about heaven will determine what kind of a life you will embrace here on earth).**

- **What have you done to personally capture God's Heart?**

- **With this knowledge of accessing heaven here on earth, in what ways can you expect your future to be different than your past?**

CONTRASTING OF
THE HEAVENS

CHAPTER 4

FIRST HEAVEN

"The Kingdom"

*"For thine is the **KINGDOM**, and the power, and the glory, forever." Amen. (Matthew 6:13b)*

"And when he was demanded of the Pharisees, when the kingdom of God should come, he answered them and said, The kingdom of God cometh not with observation: Neither shall they say, Lo here! Or, lo there! For, behold the kingdom of God is within you" (Luke 17:20-21).

We have established that there are three heavens, the lowest of which is the first. First Heaven atmosphere is a response to spiritual influence. It is therefore the dimension of the seen…the realm we can touch and feel. The chair that I sit in; the car that I drive, the clothes that I wear; all these material things are in the locale of First Heaven sensory. First Heaven is an atmospheric heaven, specifically the atmosphere around the earth. It is where the birds fly and the winds blow. This is where showers, storms, mists, vapors, and clouds are formed. The sky is the place the angel was referring to in Acts 1:11 when he asked the disciples why they were "*gazing up into heaven.*" Jesus, when He was talking to His Father, "lifted up His eyes to heaven" (John 17:1) or toward the sky. This is also the realm of manifestation and revelation. Thoughts become reality in this level of heaven; the unseen becomes visible, and the theoretical becomes accessible. John 1 tells us of a **Word** that existed from the beginning and was with God in the highest of heavens. This logos or logical existing concept eventually is called Jesus only when He manifests within the earth realm. To better understand this logic, it must be viewed in the light of the principle of threes. Stemming from the fact that God is triune in nature (Jesus, The Holy Spirit, and God), many of God's creations and Kingdom principles follow a pattern of threes.

The principle of three starts with God as the nexus for all patterns of creation. The triune nature starts with Father God (Creator of all things); Jesus Christ (the Word made flesh, the Son of God); and, The Holy Spirit (the intellect and power of God).

GOD → JESUS CHRIST → THE HOLY SPIRIT

John 1 supports the fact that all three of these facets of God were present and active in creation of heaven, earth, and all that would be made. Genesis 1 tells us that this same God made the heaven(s) and the earth. Remember that Paul substantiates the presence of more than one heaven when he referred to his experience of being caught up to Third Heaven. Therefore, First and Second Heaven must naturally exist.

FIRST HEAVEN → SECOND HEAVEN → THIRD HEAVEN

After creating the heavens and the earth, this magnificent God makes man in His own image and likeness. The image of God refers to our characteristics as spiritual beings, whereas likeness alludes to the similitude of God's triune nature. When God made Adam, he was formed of the dust of the ground (body), and given the breath of life (soul) and made in the image of God (spirit).

BODY → SOUL → SPIRIT

When Jesus teaches His disciples to pray, He declares that the Kingdom, power, and glory all belong to God.

KINGDOM → POWER → GLORY

The connection of these principles with the principle of threes is not readily seen until all of these components are put together.

FIRST HEAVEN → SECOND HEAVEN → THIRD HEAVEN
GOD → JESUS CHRIST → THE HOLY SPIRIT
BODY → SOUL → SPIRIT
KINGDOM → POWER → GLORY

From creation, it would seem that God designed First Heaven to be the manifestation of Third Heaven concepts and mandates. Jesus taught His disciples to pray that God's will be done on earth as it is in heaven. Jesus was the physical manifestation of God and His intentional relationship with man; the body carries out the thoughts and desires held within the spirit of man; the Kingdom of God is the ultimate earthly expression of God's glory. In essence, Jesus, flesh, and Kingdom are all First Heaven terms and manifestations. When Jesus declared that the *Kingdom, power, and glory* belonged to God, He was making the ultimate declaration of God's Sovereignty. So in understanding First Heaven, what exactly is Kingdom?

The Greek word for kingdom is *entos*, meaning in the midst. The Kingdom in its outward form had been rejected by the Jews. During this present age it will not come with observation, but in the hearts of the believer. It was actually in the midst of the Pharisees in the person of the King and his disciples as it is in our midst. The presence of a Kingdom implies the actualization of the existence of a king. The body has a role to play in the manifestation of the Kingdom of God coming. If not, Jesus would not have instructed us to pray "thy Kingdom come."

Therefore, it must not be assumed to manifest automatically. The believer is the vessel that the Father will use to manifest the Kingdom on earth.

The kingdom of heaven is in the earthly sphere of the universal Kingdom of God. The two have many things in common and in some contexts the terms are interchangeable. Like the kingdom of heaven, the Kingdom of God is realized in the rule of God in the present age and will also be fulfilled in the future millennial Kingdom. It continues forever in the eternal state. The Kingdom of God is also used to designate the sphere of salvation entered only by the new birth (John 3:5-7) in contrast with the kingdom of heaven as the sphere of profession, which may be real or false.

> *"And I saw a new heaven and a new earth; for the* <u>*First Heaven*</u> *and the first earth were passed away; and there was no more sea" (Revelations 21:1).*

> *"Since we consider and look not to the things that are seen but to the things that are unseen; for the things that are visible are temporal (brief*

and fleeting), but the things that are invisible are deathless and everlasting"(2 Corinthians 4:18).

Paul lets us know that the things that are visible to the naked human eye are things that are temporary and fleeting. These are the things that won't last; yet this is the realm that most Christians choose to dwell in. We get hung up on what things "look like" and react to situations as they appear. For the believer, to whom faith must be paramount, this is the place where we settle. The doctor gives us daunting health reports and our immediate response is to operate in fear, as if there is no hope of change; settling. The trick of the enemy is to make you so consumed and distracted with First Heaven visible issues that you never stretch to reach for Third Heaven. If First Heaven is the realm of manifestation, then it is clearly not the beginning or source of the matter. In fact in Kingdom, once things have manifested or appeared on earth (First Heaven), it is usually at the end of its cycle and requires a First Heaven reaction in order to be altered. Relegating yourself to First Heaven responses makes you reactionary, at best. However, you were never built to be reactionary, but an initiator! Consider again the fact that God made man in His likeness, to be just like Him. When God was creating the Heavens and the earth, He was not reacting but initiating what He desired to see. Even when we consider the fact that Jesus was already in motion as a part of God's plan before Adam and Eve sinned, it prompts us to understand that this action of God's was not reactionary but preemptive. You were not meant to be relegated to settling for whatever life hands you. You are an initiator. Your heritage can be traced from creation to that of a conqueror and starter. The antidote to dealing with First Heaven visible issues is to preempt each tactic by dwelling in a higher realm called Third Heaven. You may physically live in First Heaven, but your mentality, residence, and spiritual hope should abide and rule from Third Heaven. Dwelling on the plane of Third Heaven allows the occupant to see things before they manifest, and equips us to adequately deal with them. Essentially this is what discernment is: seeing things as they really are from the source. When we live in First Heaven but think and rule from a Third Heaven point of view, we are able to strategically preempt every attack from the kingdom of darkness. Why is this? Essentially it is because we are able to discern the true source of the situation that we face. Scary doctor reports are the perfect situations to glare past the diagnosis and live out the reality of wholeness, peace, and healing that God already foreordained the believer to walk in. In essence we are commanding the narrative and initiating our rights to have dominion in the earth. Stop waiting for life to happen to you, and command First Heaven to be your Third Heaven reality. The Word of God is full of Third Heaven realities and dictates. The Bible is God's thoughts towards the believer regarding peace, joy, life, success, and even handling failures. Your ability to withstand and initiate Third Heaven principles in a First Heaven realm hinges on how much Word you digest and live out. This is why you read your Bible, meditate on scripture, and guide your life by God's Word...that you may observe *to do* all that is written in the Word.

QUESTIONS:

- **How do I handle First Heaven issues (life's challenges)?**
- **Am I reactionary or an initiator?**
- **How consistent am I in reading my Bible?**

CHAPTER 5

SECOND HEAVEN

"The Power"

*"For thine is the kingdom, and the **POWER**, and the glory, forever." Amen. (Matthew 6:13b)*

*S*econd Heaven is called the dimension of POWER because this is the realm in which the struggle for power takes place. First Heaven is reactionary, responding to the dictates of the higher heavens. So usually the conflict is between Third Heaven mandates and Second Heaven desires. It is a battle of wills that you are able to understand more than you realize. Remember the last time you were on a fast? Your spirit man initiated the fast because you were prompted by God (a Spirit) to fast for deliverance. Your spirit man desires to fast so that it can see God's will manifested in the earth (First Heaven). However, you are not just a spirit and a body, you also possess a soul (Second Heaven). While on your way to work you pass Krispy Kreme donuts, and the light is on alerting you to a new fresh batch of hot goodness ready to melt in your mouth. Well at the sight of this store you now have an alternate desire from your soul, to eat this donut…just one. So while your Spirit man wants to please God, your soul wants to satisfy its own desires based upon what your eyes beheld! Soul and Spirit are at odds, and now the battle of control between your Third Heaven mandate (fast) and Second Heaven desire (eat) has begun. Each side is trying to control First Heaven to produce *its* intended will. These power plays happen all the time, and are employed in every decision we have to make. Paul covers this battle in Romans 7 when he speaks of the *good* that he desires to do, yet the bad that he ends up living out. We walk around every day with this internal opposition that seeks to control our flesh. Most days it is a coin toss on which *will* will win. This is exactly the relationship that Second and Third Heaven experience. The good news is that you have an important role to play in determining which side wins the power struggle.

"Then he said to me, Fear not, Daniel, for from the first day that you set your mind and heart to understand and to humble yourself before your God, your words were heard, and I have come as a consequence of [and in response to] your words" (Daniel 10:12) .

Through this scripture, we can see that Daniel had been praying and fasting for 21 days. However, there was interference between where he was (First Heaven) and where his spiritual blessing was (Third Heaven). The delay was in the spiritual realm between the first and Third Heaven. This dimension is called Second Heaven. This dimension is where the prince of the kingdom of Persia withstood Michael, the archangel, who had come at Daniel's request. It is only when we learn where the delay is, and what is causing the delay that we learn what power we actually have. It then becomes apparent that we have entertained something that is delaying our spiritual blessing or breakthrough. We can then effectively engage in spiritual warfare after pinpointing the source of the blockage. The Apostle Paul wrote in II Corinthians 2:11: *"Lest Satan should get an advantage of us; for we are not ignorant of his devices."* So then, what are Satan's devices? What are the tools that he employs to sway me to his side of the struggle? Overall his predominate device is iniquity, or sin. It's funny that in today's generation we have a hard time defining adequately this three-letter word. Is sin wearing a short skirt, fishnet stockings, and pumps while entering the club? Is it simply murder, or the homicidal thought? Is sin sleeping with your neighbor's wife, or does it extend to dreaming of sleeping with her? After all, Jesus extended the definition of adultery to include the lusting in the heart [Matthew 5:28 KJV]. Sin can mean various things to various people, and there is a multitude of things that can be classified as sin. For the purposes of this book, I want to look at sin in subjective terms, based on fellowship with God. James writes, *"therefore to him that knoweth to do good, and doeth it not, to him it is sin."[4:17 KJV]* While we would like a tell-all list of the things that are deemed universally "sinful," James chooses to nuance a different perspective. In my years as a Pastor I have found that often times those who are looking for this universal list are motivated by a quest to see how close they can get to the line without really crossing it. The problem with this pursuit is that this Christian life should be lived stimulated by our love towards God, and not based on self-gratification or a fear of messing up. When we have constant fellowship (conversation) with God, He delights in expressing His desires to us. When we hear His perspective on life, we now have a personal rapport of what He deems appropriate and inappropriate for our unique and individual lives. So sin therefore, is based upon disobedience to instructions that He personally enumerates to an individual during their time of fellowship with Him. Adequate and comprehensive standards of righteousness and sin cannot be based upon another person's experience, but on what God has disclosed through fellowship. After all, if we truly love God, we will keep His commandments [John 14:23 KJV]. Sin is prompted by adhering to a Second Heaven desire instead of listening to a Third Heaven mandate from God. Giving respect or preference to sin or iniquity blocks our ability to effectively fellowship with God through prayer. Psalm 66:18 says, *"If I regard iniquity in my heart, the Lord will not hear me."* Remember, this is a power struggle between Second and Third Heaven for control over First Heaven, and you control the outcome. Sin is the tool the enemy uses against you, to cause you to strengthen his hand. As James so eloquently outlined, sin is birthed as a result of giving in to our own lust when we are tempted.

Lust, desire and temptation are examples of Second Heaven or soulish realm terms. Your soul is the seat of your emotions and desires. Anger, sensuality, bitterness, happiness and pride are all emotions that are inherently under the control of the soul. Things like patience, forgiveness, love, and mercy are all spirit-controlled attributes. When a coworker pushes your buttons by slandering your name in front of your boss a power struggle for control is employed. Do you get even and give them a piece of your mind, or do you choose to forgive and love. The pathway of sin is to get you to respond to temptation by feeding the soulish realm while ignoring the dictates from your spirit man.

There isn't a decision that you make that is not prey to this constant battle for control. So when did this struggle start? The origins of this battle predate the making of the earth. Before all of the "let there be's," God formed the angels and the heavenly host. This creative God didn't just create these hosts, but there was a hierarchical system that was perfectly based on unity and alignment under Him. There were angels divided under archangels, segmented with specific assignments and tasks. Have you ever heard of the terms *ministering* angels and *warring* angels? These are examples of the systematic arrangement that God had fashioned. Lucifer was one of these archangels with power and authority. His direct superior was God Himself; and the entire heavenly host dwelt together in Third Heaven. One day, given over to pride, Lucifer incited a rebellion against God resulting in the fall of him and his subordinates from heaven. Where did he fall? Did he fall to the earth to reside there for eternity? No, he now dwells in Second Heaven. Ephesians 2:2 calls him the "prince of the power of the air;" John 12:31 describes him as the "prince of this world;" and Ephesians 6:12 speaks of "spiritual wickedness in high places." If he is the prince of both the air and the world, then it stands to reason that currently his place of preferred rule is in the air. It is also no accident that he is called a prince but never a king. He is given attributes of one who has considerable influence but not ultimate power. In essence he is given just enough power to trump the earth, but not enough to ascend to God's throne; he dwells in Second Heaven. God gives a mandate that is meant to be implemented in First Heaven, and immediately Satan sends out a competing directive from Second Heaven causing conflict and turbulence. Contrary winds produce storms and tornados that produce anxiety, uneasiness, and an inability to be stable. Remember, as Christians we are meant to be initiators and not reactionary. However, unstable and unsettled people cannot rule or initiate anything. Through sin, the enemy's tactic is to block your connectivity to God, and subject you to his inordinate wills and desires.

> Ezekiel 8:1-3 states: *"And it came to pass in the sixth year, the sixth month, in the fifth day of the month, as I sat in mine house, and the elders of Judah sat before me, that the hand of the Lord God fell there upon me. (2) Then I beheld, and lo a likeness as the appearance of fire: from the appearance f his loins even upward, as the appearance of brightness, as the color of amber. (3) And he put forth the form of a hand, and took me by a lock of mine head; and the spirit lifted me up between the earth and the heaven, and brought me in the visions of God to Jerusalem, to the door*

of the inner gate that looketh toward the north; where was the seat of the image of jealousy, which provoketh to jealousy."

In Ezekiel's vision, the Hand of the Lord lifted him up between the earth (First Heaven) and the heaven (Third Heaven). In this Second Heaven dimension, Ezekiel saw the spirit of jealousy, which was in operation in Second Heaven causing corruption in the temple located in First Heaven. This spirit of jealousy caused idolatry to manifest itself in the people in the temple. Today, the Church has given away much of her authority to Satan because of ignorance. He has created much havoc and has caused iniquity to abound. Consequently, the Church has become a sleeping limp giant.

Second Heaven is a highly organized dimension with much power. So the question then is: "Can we as believers ever penetrate this dimension to get a breakthrough to the place where our spiritual blessings reside?" If "we wrestle not against flesh and blood, but against principalities and power,... and against spiritual wickedness in high places,..." (Ephesians 6:12). Do we have the advantage or disadvantage? We should have an understanding of the strategies, power and organization of the enemy if we are expected to fight the good fight of faith. In order to understand our position, we have to understand the origin of our opponent and why he is our opponent.

Lucifer was one of the archangels along with Gabriel and Michael. He was "in Eden, the garden of God" "upon the holy mountain of God" and "walked…..in the midst of the stones of fire" and was "created" by God. He was in heaven with God as mentioned in Isaiah 14:12:

> *"How art thou fallen from heaven, O Lucifer, son of the morning! How art thou cut down to the ground, which didst weaken the nations?"*

He fell to the ground (earth) because iniquity was found in him. Isaiah 14:13: *"For thou has said in thine heart, I will ascend into heaven, I will exalt my throne above the stars of God: I will sit also upon the mount of the congregation, in the sides of the north: (14) I will ascend above the heights of the clouds; I will be like the most High."*

Lucifer was speaking from a position looking up towards the heavens. He wanted to be in a position above the stars of God or angels and above the clouds that is above Third Heaven. He opposes man so much because he knows that Third Heaven is a place of authority, power and glory. He understands that it was created for man to live in eternally. He actually wants to hurt God by defeating man because he knows that man is the apple of God's eye. If not, then why would "God so love the world that He gave His only begotten Son" for mankind? The earth has become the battleground. The war actually took place in heaven according to Revelation 12:7:

> *"And there was war in heaven: Michael and his angels fought against the dragon; and the dragon fought and his angels. (8) and prevailed not; neither was their place found any more in heaven. (9) And the great dragon was cast out, that old serpent, called the Devil, and Satan, which deceiveth the whole world: he was cast out into the earth, and his angels were cast out with him."*

This planet became the war zone and man became entangled in warfare. Revelation 12:17:

> *"And the dragon was wroth with the woman, and went to make war with the remnant of her seed, which keep the commandments of God, and have the testimony of Jesus Christ."*

Spiritual Warfare

One of the chief difficulties of living for God today is an invisible war called spiritual warfare. As Christians, we are all engaged in this invisible battle. Our enemies are demons, *"For we are not wrestling with flesh and blood [contending only with physical opponents], but against the despotisms, against the powers, against [the master spirits who are] the world rulers of this present darkness, against the spirit forces of wickedness in the heavenly {supernatural) sphere."* [Ephesians 6:12 Amplified] The phrases… against power, …against the master spirits, …the world rulers of this present darkness, …against the spirit forces refers to demons and the power of the unseen world – Second Heaven. Even in Second Heaven battles, a No-Fly

Zone protects us. A no-fly zone is a territory over which aircraft are not permitted to fly. Such zones are usually set up in a military context, somewhat like a demilitarized zone in the sky and usually prohibit military aircraft of a belligerent nation from operating in the region. It is an area, usually the frontier or boundary between two or more military powers (or alliances), where military activity is not permitted, usually by peace treaty, armistice, or other bilateral or multilateral agreement. When the prayers of the righteous ascend into Second Heaven, a no-fly zone is created over the people of God. Third Heaven promise is then able to pass through Second Heaven and rest on First Heaven. In military terms, a demilitarized zone (DMZ) is created.

A great example of this is found in the life of Job. Job was said to have been a perfect and upright man who feared God and eschewed evil. Satan asked for permission to test Job by taking his substance, children, and his body. God gave him permission to test Job BUT with a limitation… "Only upon himself put not forth thine hand." That was the NO FLY ZONE! As we gain access to Second Heaven, there is still a place within us that is protected by God himself! Glory to God! So whatever happens to us has to be permitted by God. Hardships, hard times, failures, etc. are not meant to take us out, but to strengthen us. Our Heavenly Father knows the strength and the power that is within us. He also knows our limitations, so therefore he has placed a No-Fly Zone strategically around us that cannot be permeated.

Part of the struggle between maintaining a First and Second Heaven lifestyle, particularly as it relates to the Christian life, is to be able to recognize our enemies' strategies against our forward momentum, and to know how to make our stands on a spiritual instead of a carnal level. This condition is the reason behind the apostolic imperative, *"Put on God's whole armor [the armor of a heavy-armed soldier which God supplies], that you may be able successfully to stand up against [all] the strategies and the deceits of the devil"* (Ephesians 6:11). Without spiritual help from God, the Christian is unable to win in this spiritual battle.

Our position is one of authority! We (you and I) are seated together in heavenly places with Christ Jesus far above Second Heaven. Once we realize who we are in Christ Jesus, we can better operate from that position of authority within that realm. We must realize that we already have the advantage.

Second Heaven can influence man's emotions in three areas of temptation: the lust of the eyes; lust of the flesh; and the pride of life. Satan is always recruiting men and women to operate in the realm of Second Heaven in order to abort their progress. You are on track to fulfillment of your destiny. Misunderstandings, pride, indifference, jealousy, fear, impatience, forgiveness, a critical attitude, insensitivity, inconsistency, double-mindedness, vanity and hypocrisy are types of Second Heaven attitudes that can halt progression and cause loss of time and setbacks. Overcoming them with trust, humility, concern, respect, understanding, unity, etc. are aspects that can bring Third Heaven manifestation to First Heaven.

CHAPTER 6
THIRD HEAVEN

"Glory"

*"For thine is the Kingdom, and the power, and the **GLORY**, forever. Amen"(Matthew 6:13b).*

2 Corinthians 12:2-3: "I know a man in Christ who fourteen years ago – whether in the body or out of the body I do not know, God knows – was caught up to the <u>third heaven</u>. And I know that this man – whether in the body or away from the body I do not know, God knows—was caught up into paradise, and he heard utterances beyond the power of man to put into words, which man is not permitted to utter."

*A*lthough the "Third Heaven" is not mentioned in the Genesis narrative, the established structure of all things is defined in Genesis 1. When understood, it allows us to comprehend exactly where and what Paul was talking about when he mentions the "Third Heaven" in his letter. It also gives the reader a better understanding of John's vision in Revelation 4. Again, when the Lord God divided the waters He created a boundary that presently exists between the two lower heavens (which constitute the firmament) and Third Heaven (where the throne of God is).

Colossians 3:1-3: *"If then you have been raised with Christ [to a new life, thus sharing His resurrection from the dead], aim at and seek the [rich, eternal treasures] that are above, where Christ is, seated at the right hand of God. (Psalm 110:1) And set your minds and keep them set on what is above (the higher things), not on the things that are on the earth. For [as far as this world is concerned] you have died, and your [new, real] life is hidden with Christ in God."* [Amplified Bible]

Third Heaven is perfect purity, and God wants to purify His saints on earth so they will enjoy heaven's atmosphere. Third Heaven is fullness of joy, and God desires to give joy to His people on earth. Third Heaven is everlasting freedom, and God longs for His people to have deliverance while on earth. Third Heaven is perfect wholeness, and God wants to heal His people here on earth. Third Heaven is complete security, and God wants His people to feel confident and secure here on earth. Heaven is fruition and fulfillment, and God desires that His people be fulfilled on earth. When Jesus instructed us to pray that God's will be done on earth as it is in heaven (Matthew 6:10), He revealed that God wants us to have a taste of Third Heaven here on earth!

The Lord has storehouses of blessings just for us. They are waiting in the Third Heaven realm for you to access them, and to receive them now, here in First Heaven. Healing is waiting for people on earth. The day will come when there will be an avalanche of miracles and healings manifesting here on the earth. God's power is waiting to be released! But we must do it when we take dominion. Dominion is a Kingdom term. God gave us dominion indicating that He is King Himself. He is therefore able to give domino power to whomever He decides. He has given this power to us!

> Genesis 1:26 : *"And God said let us [Father, Son, and Holy Spirit] make mankind in Our image, after Our likeness, and let them have complete authority **(dominion)** over the fish and over the fowl of the air and over the cattle, over everything creeping think that creepeth upon the earth."*

Every Kingdom has dominion and established protocol. Protocol is a code prescribing strict adherence to correct etiquette and procedure. God is our King. His Kingdom is called heaven. The Lord's throne is in heaven. The earth is His footstool. He is the King of earth as well as heaven. God gave dominion to Adam. As long as he followed God's protocol, he was able to stay in the Garden of Eden, God's place of blessing. He could relate to God and God could relate to him. It was called fellowship.

The enemy's agenda is to create chaos and to stop God's Third Heaven protocol through broken fellowship. Protocol is important. When there is a breach of protocol, it must be dealt with. Lucifer created a breach of protocol, and God had to deal with him. Proper protocol leads to intimacy. Wherever there is intimacy, there is communication leading to revelation. Revelation leads to manifestation. In the Garden, God was trying to teach Adam that if you say what I say and do what I say do, then whatever you say will be established. Adam saw the animals, and named them. There wasn't any confusion or impurity in the atmosphere, so Adam is speaking from the heavenlies and naming the animals what God names them. Protocol is being followed and manifestation occurs. This revelation is more important than money or things. Revelation is the key to manifestation and dominion.

Cain broke protocol when it came to giving; therefore, God didn't have any respect or regard for his offering. Cain wanted to break protocol, and offer unto God what he wanted with the expectation of the same reward as his brother. When he found out that his offering wasn't acceptable, Cain became angry and indignant. He looked sad, dejected and depressed. Depression, dejection and sadness are sometimes the result of not following God's protocol for our lives. These feelings are released from

Second Heaven (our soulish realm). If the Holy Spirit does not lead us, these feelings manifest in a First Heaven (or earthly/ physical realm). The result is a bad attitude, bad disposition, broken relationships, etc. God began to explain to Cain that if you do well, (or follow what I am saying to you), you will be accepted. If you do not, sin crouches at your door. He says sin's desire is for you, but you must master it. In order to master sin in our lives, we must follow the leading of the Holy Spirit, which allows us to follow God's protocol. God's protocol is the Third Heaven way of dealing with the sin and temptations that crouch at our door.

The Will of God

The Will of God is found in the Mind of God. When man receives revelation of his purpose and future, good manifestation begins to take place. It is then that man is at his strongest in the earth. God's Will becomes evident, and we begin to see success in the earthly realm. It must be frustrating to demons (after they have accomplished some evil scheme) to later find out that they were carrying out the Will of God. Satan did not realize what God wanted to do in Job's life when he caused him physical suffering. Also, God used "an evil spirit" to accomplish His Will in the life of Saul, Israel's first king (1 Sam. 16:14). On another occasion, God used "a lying spirit" to deceive the false prophets of the evil king, Ahab (1 Kings 22:22-23). At the end of the Great Tribulation, demons will be used by God to gather the nations of the world to the battlefield of Armageddon (Revelation 9:16). God is able to use even demons to accomplish His Will. So don't become discouraged when trials come your way as you progress towards a Third Heaven lifestyle. Remember, God will cause all things to work together for your good.

CHAPTER 7
ACCESSING THIRD HEAVEN

Third Heaven Laws

$\mathscr{E}$ very kingdom has laws. We need laws in society, so our society can regulate and work properly. They are designed to protect us, our property and to ensure that everyone in society behaves the way that the community expects. Without laws there would be complete anarchy. So it is with the kingdom of heaven. In order for man to access protection and work properly in the Kingdom, there are laws that have been enacted that we must follow. Imagine if there were no laws. There would be utter chaos! What is decided to be positive in one environment (and acceptable); may not be in another. What we do as a family, or group when gathered in the same atmosphere, is the very process of creating a climate conducive for empowerment.

The laws of Third Heaven are:

Third Heaven Law of Decision Making;

(1) Third Heaven Law of Enduring Silence;

(2) Third Heaven Law of Praying;

(3) Third Heaven Law of True Forgiveness;

(4) Third Heaven Law of Enduring Temptation;

(5) Third Heaven Law of Wisdom;

(6) Third Heaven Law of Will Alignment; and

(7) Third Heaven Law of Unity.

The dos and don'ts of our climate (and the requests that we make) are the ways in which a positive atmosphere for each of us as individuals is not only created, but also maintained for the benefit of everyone. Through the process of Third Heaven choices on behalf of everyone – we are creating a place to live, work, play and learn that is a gift not only in the present, but for those to follow in the future. In order to maintain a positive atmosphere for progress, each individual must choose to comply with (and even be obedient to specific requests), enforced rules, or laws that are designated by those within a specific area or atmosphere. The choice is ours.

Third Heaven Law of Decision Making
"Making Proper Decisions"

Genesis 14:18-24: *"And Melchizedek king of Salem brought forth bread and wine: and he was the priest of the most high God. And he blessed him, and said, Blessed be Abram of the most high God, possessor of heaven and earth: And blessed be the most high God, which hath delivered thine enemies into thy hand. And he gave him tithes of all. And the king of Sodom said unto Abram, Give me the persons, and take the goods to thyself. And Abram said to the king of Sodom, I have lift up mine hand unto the LORD, the most high God, the possessor of heaven and earth, That I will not take from a thread even to a shoelatchet, and that I will not take any thing that is thine, lest thou shouldest say, I have made Abram rich: Save only that which the young men have eaten, and the portion of the men which went with me, Aner, Eschcol, and Mamre; let them take their portion."*

Abram is given the mandate to leave his country, his people and his father's household and go to a land that "I shall show you" in Genesis 12:1. He leaves his father's house, after setting things in order. He left, but he decided to take his nephew Lot with him, which means he made a decision to partially obey God. Partial obedience is the same as disobedience. It can also become a roadblock to your destiny.

As a result quarreling broke out between the herdsmen of Abram and Lot because of the massive wealth both had. They were also surrounded by the Canaanites and Perizzites, their enemies (Second Heaven). Being surrounded by hostile neighbors, the herdsmen of Abram and Lot should have pulled together and united as one. Instead, they let petty jealousy tear them apart. Similar situations exist today. We often bicker while Satan is at work among believers. Rivalries, arguments, and disagreements among believers can be especially destructive in four ways: (1) they damage goodwill, trust, and peace – the foundations of good human relations; (2) they hamper progress toward important goals; (3) they make us self-centered rather than love-centered; and (4) they cause us to be labeled hypocrites by those who are looking on. Petty disagreements and arguments among believers are designed to keep the believer trapped in a dimension called "First Heaven." This is a place where one gets distracted and is led by feelings, sight and emotions, which is indicative of the sensory realm. This is the realm that the Apostle Paul called temporal—the things that are seen. In this realm, arguments among brothers become very destructive. In John 17:21 Jesus prays that His followers be "one." This is a third dimensional prayer because it requires moving past oneself in engaging in petty arguments and disagreements in order to operate in a higher place defined as oneness. Lot's character is revealed in this dimension by his choices. He took the best share of the land even though it meant living near Sodom, a city known for its sin. His greed made him want the best for himself, without thinking about the needs of his uncle Abram, his family or generations to come. First dimension thinking always thinks about what will benefit ME, and not the betterment of others. Life presents a series of choices. We, too, can choose the best while ignoring the needs and feelings of others. These choices lead to eventual problems for the decision-maker as well as all those who are affected by his decisions.

Good pasture and available water seemed like a wise choice to Lot at first. But he failed to recognize that wicked Sodom could potentially provide temptations strong enough to destroy his family and thus his own happiness and peace. Even though he may have felt he was strong enough to resist temptations, other members of his family and those in his community may not have been. Sometimes, we will be given the option of making choices in which we can handle the consequences, but third dimensional thinking goes beyond us and considers whether or not our choices will cause others to fail. When others fail, because we are one, then we fail, too!

In Genesis 19:1, Lot is sitting at the gate of Sodom. When one is seated, it is indicative of a position of authority. He is in a position in that land where he sanctions the goings on in that community. The town has to be destroyed because of the sin that he has allowed.

Lot's greedy desire for the best of everything led him into sinful surroundings. His burning desire for possessions and success cost him his freedom and enjoyment. As a captive to Kadorlaomer, he faced torture, slavery, or death. This was First Heaven decision-making at its finest. In much the same way, we can be enticed into doing things or going places we shouldn't. The prosperity we long for is captivating. It can both entice us and enslave us if our motives are not in line with God's desires.

Alternatively, Abram was prepared to come to Lot's assistance. Because of his faith in God, Abram was willing and empowered to free his nephew. This incident portrays two of Abram's Third Heaven characteristics: (1) He had courage that came from God. Facing a powerful foe, when attacked, and (2) he was prepared. He had taken time to train his men for a potential conflict. We never know when we will be called upon to complete difficult tasks. Like Abram, Third Heaven thinking always prepares for those times and takes courage from God when they come. When Abram learned that Lot was a prisoner, he immediately tried to rescue his nephew. It would have been easier and safer for Abram not to become involved. But with Lot in serious trouble, Abram acted at once. Sometimes we must get involved in a messy or painful situation in order to help others. We should be willing to act immediately when others need our help. Lot's story gives us hope that God forgives, and often brings about positive circumstances from evil.

These points (taken from Abraham and Lot's experiences) are the keys to making effective Third Heaven decisions and sticking with them:

(1) Make a Third Heaven decision. If you don't make the decision, someone or something else will.

(2) Withdraw from the negative influences that would interfere with your decision. Negative influences will take you off course. Jesus withdrew at times, and so should we.

(3) Pray and fast during the process. You will need His guidance from Third Heaven in order to stay focused on the decision and not the circumstances.

(4) Obey the leading of the Holy Spirit during the process. There will be times that God will release direction or strategies along the way. Obey what you believe He is saying. He knows what you don't.

(5) Make a declaration of the decision in order that it may manifest from Third Heaven to First Heaven. This brings about accountability and changes the atmosphere to one where manifestation can occur.

QUESTIONS:

- **What is the direction of your life?**

- **Are you headed toward God or away from Him?**

- **Are you drifting between two different directions in life? If you're a drifter the choice for God may seem difficult, but it is the one choice that puts all other choices in a different light.**

- **Are you willing to go beyond yourself and step into oneness with God?**

- **Do you operate mostly in the First Heaven realm or the Third Heaven realm?**

- **What Third Heaven choices have you made recently?**

- **What First Heaven choices have you made that you regret?**

Third Heaven Law of Enduring Silence

Revelation 8:1 "And when he had opened the seventh seal, there was silence in heaven about the space of half an hour."

What do we do when God is silent? Sometimes we tend to think that we have done something wrong, and He is punishing us by not speaking. True relationships understand that silence is part of fellowship. Just to be sitting in the presence of someone we love without them speaking a word can indicate the enjoyment of them being near. The scripture says that there was silence in heaven for about half an hour. With all the activity, this dramatic pause must have seemed to last for an eternity. When God is silent, it does seem like an eternity. As a people, we tend to be uncomfortable with silence. The reason is that we are uncomfortable with ourselves and our inner most thoughts. A flurry of activity tends to drown out the need to become one with God. We must seek God in times of silence. How proper for us to be quiet and honor God for His power and might. Take time each day to be silent and exalt God. Silence also conveys trust and confidence in God [*see* Isaiah 30:15]. We can trust God that He will give us strength and provide the justice against oppressors that we seek.

> *Psalm 38:13-14: "...I am like a deaf man, who cannot hear, like a mute, who cannot open his mouth; I have become like a man who does not hear, whose mouth can offer no reply."*

Being silent can be extremely difficult when others tear us down because we want to protect our reputation. We find it difficult to do nothing while they assault something so precious to us. But we don't need to lash back in revenge or justify our position; we can trust God to protect our reputation. Jesus was silent before His accusers (Luke 23:9, 10); He left His case in God's Hands (1 Peter 2:21-24). That is a good place to leave our case, too!

In Psalm 39:1-3, David resolved to keep his tongue from sin; that is, he decided not to complain to other people about God's treatment of him. David certainly had reason to complain. He was the anointed king of Israel, but he had to wait many years before taking the throne. Then one of his sons tried to kill him to become king instead. But when David could not keep still any longer, he took his complaints directly to God. We all have complaints about our jobs, money, or situations, but complaining to others may make them think that God cannot take care of us. It may also look as if we blame God for our troubles. Instead, like David, we should take our complaints directly to God. He can take it.

God warned Judah that turning to Egypt and other nations for military strength could not save them. Only God could do that. They must wait for Him in "quietness and trust." No amount of fast-talking or hasty activity could speed up God's grand design. We have nothing to say to God, but THANK YOU! Salvation comes from God, alone. Because He has saved us, we can trust Him and be peacefully confident that He will give us strength to face our difficulties. We should lay aside our busy care (and endless effort), and allow Him to act.

It is in the silence that God truly speaks. When we get quiet before God, He will give direction from the Third Heaven. We must learn to silence our minds, our souls and our spirits through focusing all that we are on our Heavenly Father. Sometimes our thoughts and our emotions are still rambling on even when we are trying to hear from God. It is at these moments that our thoughts and emotions (disguising themselves as coming from God) want to take over to control our actions. This is the Second Heaven activity that must be quieted down in order to hear, accurately and clearly, from the Third Heaven. I know that it is hard to shut down and endure the silence. You must believe when God begins to break the silence and speak, it is well worth it! Silence must be practiced over and over again until it becomes a way of life. After all, effective communication is two-way, not just one person doing all of the talking while the other person does all the listening.

QUESTIONS:

- When is the last time you got silent before God?

- What struggles did you experience in quieting your thoughts and emotions to get quiet before Him?

- What First Heaven situations have you endured in silence?

- Name the emotions that were the driving force behind the breaking of the silence. Reputation, Pride, Jealousy, Envy, Bitterness, Insecurity....

- If any of these drove you to break the silence, identify them as First, Second or Third Heaven responses.

- Did complaining enhance the situation?

- When God is silent, what should our correct response be?

- Write down what you believe you heard God speak?

Third Heaven Law of Praying

Matthew 6:9: "When you pray, pray like this "Our Father, which are in heaven, hallowed be thy name, thy kingdom come, thy will be done, on earth as it is in heaven, give us this day, our daily bread, forgive us our debts as we forgive our debtors, lead us not into temptation, but deliver us from evil, for thine is the kingdom, and the power, and the glory forever, amen.""

Prayer is a necessity if you are going to access Third Heaven. It is the language of the heart of man to the Heart of God. It is the conversation of the Kingdom. Praying in the Spirit is Third Heaven praying. Praying in the fleshly realm is First Heaven praying and praying in the soulish realm is Second Heaven praying. Jesus said in John 4:24: *"God is a Spirit, and they that worship him must worship him in Spirit and in truth."* Spirit-to-Spirit communication is effective praying. My question to you is: Do your prayers reach Third Heaven or are they hung up in Second Heaven?

In Matthew 6:5-8 Jesus instructed His disciples to pray in this manner: *"And when you come before God, don't turn that into a theatrical production either. All these people making a regular show out of their prayers, hoping for stardom! Do you think God sits in a box seat? Here's what I want you to do: Find a quiet, secluded place so you won't be tempted to role-play before God. Just be there as simply and honestly as you can manage. The focus will shift from you to God, and you will begin to sense his grace. The world is full of so-called prayer warriors who are prayer igno-rant. They're full of formulas and programs and advice, peddling techniques for getting what you want from God. Don't fall for that nonsense. This is your Father you are dealing with, and he knows better than you what you need. With a God like this loving you, you can pray very simply." [The Message Bible]*

Prayer should be persistent, and it should be intercessory. There is power in praying for others. Most prayers are selfish and self-centered. Self-centeredness, which is our original sin and the source of all actual sin, keeps our prayers locked up in the Second Heaven or soulish realm. The remedy for self-centeredness is to intercede for others persistently. It looses the Hand of God to work on your behalf. This selfless act aligns your prayer life with that of the prayer life of Jesus. As Jesus prayed for His disciples, it released Him to His Third Heaven destiny. The same applies to us. When we pray for others with the same fervor and intensity that we would pray for ourselves, our purpose and destinies also become manifest.

At times, there are present and past situations, hurts, forgiveness, character flaws, etc. that we need to deal with if we are going to pray effectively. These situations sometimes leave open doors that allow the enemy to come in and intercept our Third Heaven prayers. Once you allow God to point out any open doors in your life, agree to close them with the help of the Holy Spirit. Genesis 28 is a prime example of Jacob's Third Heaven dreams and experience once he allowed God to change his character. Before then, he lived the life of a trickster. He inherited this lifestyle from his mother and Uncle Laban. It was a generational curse that needed to be broken. He tricked his father and his brother out of his brother's birthright and blessing. The cycle continued and his Uncle Laban eventually tricked him for 14 years. In order for the curse to be broken, Jacob had to admit to God that he was indeed a trickster and ask for forgiveness from his brother. Curses are spiritual cycles that perpetuate themselves throughout generations. Since they are spiritual in nature, they must be broken by spiritual means. During this process Jacob has a dream and sees a vision of angels ascending and descending from heaven. He gains a greater revelation (and curses are destroyed) because he allowed God to point out and shut the open doors in his life. Accessing the Third Heaven gives spiritual revelation and strategies for breaking curses and closing doors that might have been present for generations!

Praying Your Watch

"Oh, I know, I have been rash to talk out plainly this way to God!] I will [in my thinking] stand upon my post of observation and station myself

on the tower or fortress, and will watch to see what He will say within me and what answer I will make [as His mouthpiece] to the perplexities of my complaint against Him." [Habakkuk 2:1 Amplified Bible]

Habakkuk wanted to be in the best position to receive God's direction. He understood that in his life, he was assigned a specific post or watch. He knew that if he stayed on his particular watch, God would speak to him in his inner man (in his Third Heaven place). It is very important that we adhere to God's Voice for direction because He speaks from a Third Heaven place. We must remain sensitive within our inner man to hear from Him. And some of you may find that you are called to specific prayer times just as Daniel or Habakkuk.

There are eight prayer watches described in the Bible. At times in your life, you may sense that you are being awakened at a specific time every day. This may be the time that God wants to commune with you by Himself in prayer. Everyone is assigned a watch. At different seasons in your life, you may find that your prayer watch time changes. Know this: every watch has an assigned purpose depending on what God is speaking to your heart.

6 a.m. to 9 a.m. This is usually the time that God calls you to strengthen you.

9 a.m. to noon. This is usually the time for strengthening of relationships through healing of broken relationships.

Noon to 3 p.m. This is the time to declare and release God's Third Heaven promises and strategies into manifestation. Use the power of the tongue to declare life!

3 p.m. to 6 p.m. This is the time to unmask any covered sins and ungodly motivations that are impeding your progress, your family's progress, your financial and spiritual progress, and the progress of God and His Kingdom.

6 p.m. to 9 p.m. This is the time of meditation on the Word of God and having the Word manifest inside of us; time for deliverance from carnal and Second Heaven influences; time for resurrection of dreams and purposes that have not come to pass; time to pray for the economy; time to expose and confound all the wicked structures from our economic systems, educational systems, religious systems, political systems and all other systems.

9 p.m. to midnight. This is the time for thanksgiving; time for visitation; the time when the Lord prepares you to receive many acts of change in First Heaven. Midnight is symbolic of intense darkness, but God is the light in the darkness and releases strategy during this time.

Midnight to 3 a.m. This is the time to pray for protection and strength to overcome; time for outpouring of the spirit of grace to overcome every limitation of gifts and anointing; special time for Divine governments; and time for overruling human decrees that have their origins in the Second Heaven to give an angelic release.

3 a.m. to 6 a.m. This is the time to pray for freedom of the Bride (us); Third Heaven angelic activity or intervention on our behalf; and the time when God releases the mysteries of Third Heaven. This is the time for blessings from Third Heaven above; blessings of First Heaven beneath; blessings that have been held up in Second Heaven; and blessings of our fathers and ancestors.

QUESTIONS:

- Do you sense that God is beckoning you to pray more?

- Is there a particular time that you are being led to pray every day?

- Make a list of the days and times you sense an urgency to pray.

- Is there a pattern?

- Have there been times that you have been called to pray and really don't know what or who to pray for?

- Ask the Holy Spirit to direct your prayer to move from a First Heaven (earthly) prayer to a Third Heaven prayer.

Third Heaven Law of True Forgiveness

"And forgive us our debts, as we forgive our debtors..."(Matthew 6:12).

Unforgiveness is like a seed that grows in darkness in hidden places. The darkness of the heart is where the seed germinates. These seeds can remain dormant for years or even decades. They tend to manifest themselves in anger, resentment, rebellion, retaliation, pride, jealousy, arrogance and manipulation. I speak of true forgiveness because sometimes we say that we forgive, but in our hearts, we don't truly forgive. This may show itself as behavior modification. We learn a behavior instead of dealing with the true issue at the root of the problem. Many of us have learned how to mask so many things. God is waiting for the real you to come clean, and admit there is a problem in forgiving those who we deem to have trespassed against us.

Unforgiveness becomes a stronghold in our lives. It's the place where we get stuck! It is the stumbling block that we have allowed in our lives and even given it a comfortable place in our souls. We work around it acting like it's not even there, not realizing the damage it is causing. It may be what is hindering our access to the next place in our lives. We must ask ourselves, 'Is it worth my life's progress to be stuck in this place of unforgiveness?'

You may think that you aren't hurting anybody else, but envision it this way: you see the person that you love the most drowning in a swimming pool. The water is only 3 feet deep, and you know how to swim. You can even walk over and help them, but you refuse to do it. Their life is contingent upon you making a decision whether or not to jump in to save them. There wouldn't be any harm to you, but you stay on the sidelines debating within yourself whether or not to jump in. It's just as simple as jumping in the water and bringing that loved one back to safety. Just think, you have purposely disconnected yourself from them. This is a dangerous mindset to embrace at a time in your life that may be critical to your own survival and the survival of others.

Beloved, there are generations waiting for you to jump into the water of forgiveness. Their destinies may depend on that one place of forgiveness. That's how true Third Heaven forgiveness works. Its focus is always centered on the love of others. First

Heaven forgiveness always has emotional strings attached to it. It makes statements like, "I will only forgive you if you do this or that." Remember that Second Heaven normally controls emotions unless we break free and become led by the Holy Spirit. Romans 8:14 states *"For as many as are led by the Spirit of God, they are the sons of God."* In the process of becoming the sons of God, you free yourself from the guilt of allowing a loved one to drown when you have the ability to rescue them.

Notice, I said process, which means that it may take awhile to reach the goal of truly forgiving. However, also remember that the clock is ticking and that person in the water only has so long to flail around waiting for help. The quicker you go through the process, the quicker the release to a new Third Heaven you! Learn to forgive quickly. Just take the plunge and jump in. It starts from within your spirit.

Maybe the first person you need to forgive is yourself. You are entitled to your own forgiveness and the forgiveness from our loving God! You are worth it! He died for your forgiveness. When you don't forgive, you are actually punishing yourself. Somehow we feel that if we forgive the other person, we become vulnerable. Vulnerability to God's process of true forgiveness actually strengthens you. It allows you to understand that the other person may have been doing the best they could. They may not have had the proper situations in their lives to help them manage through life. All of us have lacked in some area of our lives, and we would expect to be understood and forgiven as well. Now it's time to give the control (and the results of the situation) over to God and release the consequences to Him. How freeing! You have come too far to change course now! Stay on course to your destined place!

QUESTIONS:

- **What happened? (Describe)**

- **What I did? (Describe)**

- **What I should have done? (Third Heaven response – cite and explain references)**

- **What I now must do? (Steps that must be taken to rectify matters)**

Now take the paper that you wrote all of this on and burn it! It is gone forever!

- ## How do you feel?

Now begin to walk in your Third Heaven freedom!

Third Heaven Law of Enduring Temptation

"Lead us not into temptation but deliver us from the evil one" (Matthew 6:13).

No one can decide how he is to be tempted, only how he is to respond to temptation. It is this variable that presents a continuing challenge to constant accountability to the sufficiency of grace. One may be able to resist successfully a thousand temptations in succession while a hidden one is taking over at a lower level of awareness.

Temptation comes from evil desires inside us, not from God. It begins with a simple evil thought and becomes sin when we dwell on the thought and allow it to become an action. Like a snowball rolling downhill, sin grows more destructive the more we let it have its way. The best time to stop a temptation is before it is too strong or moving too fast to control.

The evil desire lies in the area of tempting believers to pursue a lifestyle apart from God. These evil desires influence the lost by binding them to some particular sin and convincing them that they are not worthy to become Christians. They influence

Christians into sin and convince them that they are too sinful to enjoy fellowship with Christ. Their efforts are, in a particular manner, directed against the saints (who are the objects of the evil one's envy and hatred) because they have been restored to the favor of God, and are engaged in His service. Jesus told His disciples, that Satan had desired to have them, that he might sift them as wheat. However, in Matthew 6:13 Jesus teaches us to pray *"And lead (bring) us not into temptation, but deliver us from the evil one. For Yours is the kingdom and the power and the glory forever, Amen."*

As long as one remains in the body, one is susceptible to inaccurate perceptions that lead to errors of judgment, and deceptive appearances that tend toward erroneous conclusions. We must recognize that the more we walk in Third Heaven concepts, the more we become aware of our own sinfulness and distance from the purity of Christ. As our vision becomes clearer, we can see our own imperfections more clearly.

Adam while innocent was tempted. Even Jesus who knew no sin was tempted in every way that characterizes human existence. Those whose feet are set on the path to Third Heaven living do not become free from temptation, though they grow in their ability to overcome it. There isn't any point at which they cannot make further progress in grace.

Third Heaven Law of Wisdom

Webster defines wisdom as having discernment for what is true, right or lasting, judicious; having knowledge or information; being informed, aware of. Understanding is the application of wisdom.

Wisdom is shown in getting desired ends by effective means.

Third Heaven wisdom attributes are shown forth in good works, noble living and humility. The opposite of true is false, which means that there must be more than one kind of wisdom. According to the book of James, there is also superficial wisdom, which is earthly and unspiritual. As discussed earlier, earthly is First Heaven because it is manifested in jealousy, contention, rivalry, selfish ambition, unrest, disharmony and rebellion. These are all sensual and emotional qualities that come directly from Second Heaven.

Along with praying for wisdom, one must also pray for understanding as well. The scriptures instruct us to get wisdom, but in all our getting we must get an understanding. Practical application of wisdom brings a Third Heaven revelation down to First Heaven where it can be lived out. Understanding is the instruction manual for wisdom. It is what drives the life of wise people. One can have wisdom but not know how to apply it.

First Heaven wisdom is the wisdom of the physical, visible world.

Second Heaven wisdom is the wisdom of the emotion.

Third Heaven wisdom is the wisdom that comes from above.

According to James 1:5 The Third Heaven wisdom that we need has three distinct characteristics:

(1) It is practical. An intelligent person may have profound ideas, but a wise person puts profound ideas into action. Intelligence will allow someone to describe several reasons why the car broke down. The wise person chooses the most likely reason and proceeds to take action through understanding.

(2) It is Divine. God's wisdom goes beyond common sense. Common sense does not lead us to choose joy in the middle of trials. This wisdom begins with respect for

God, leads to living by God's direction, and results in the ability to tell right from wrong.

(3) It is Christlike. Asking for wisdom is ultimately asking to be like Christ. (I Corinthians 1:24; 2:1-7)

Third Heaven Law of Will Alignment

"Thy will be done in earth, as it is in heaven..."(Matthew 6:10b).

The definition of alignment, in plain English, is to place something in a line with something else; or to arrange it so as to be parallel or straight with something else in order to function at its maximum capacity. The alignment of our will with the Will of God, allows us to bring Third Heaven to the earth and operate at our maximum capacity of greatness. In the garden, Jesus surrendered His Will to the Father when He stated "nevertheless, not my will but thy will be done." Had He not aligned His Will with that of the Father, we would still be lost, distant from God and destined for eternal separation. Jesus's purpose for coming to the earth would never have been fulfilled. Just like Jesus, we were born with a purpose. The ultimate fulfilling of our purpose depends on whether or not we are aligned with our Third Heaven purpose (God's way of doing and responding here on earth.) This is how we manifest Third Heaven here on First Heaven.

The book of James tells us that a double-minded man is unstable in all his ways. This implies that man is influenced by two different wills, the Will of God and the will of man. At any given time, we are found to be following in one or the other. We, at times, are fickle. We follow the Will of God to a certain extent, and when it becomes uncomfortable, we follow our own will. We switch between the Third Heaven Will of God, to the Second Heaven will of our emotions. This improper alignment causes us to miss the perfect Will of God for our lives. Then we settle for less and live below our potential.

We all have the tendency to sin. This does not destroy free will nor does it imply that what God has commanded is totally impossible. Yet, it does make free will vulnerable, but through proper alignment of our faith and trust in God, our will begins to align itself with God's Will. We begin to freely seek God for the strategies and direction from Third Heaven.

Third Heaven Law of Unity

Unity Allows one to Access Third Heaven –

Matthew 18:19-20: *"Again I say unto you, That if two of you shall agree on earth as touching anything that they shall ask, it shall be done for them of my Father which is in heaven. For where two or three are gathered together in my name, there am I in the midst of them."*

Division is an instrument utilized to cause us not to access Third Heaven. The unity, however, must be attained on earth or First Heaven. Sometimes things that are seen cause stumbling blocks to unity. The sensory realm (emotions) also can be a hindrance to Third Heaven access.

The Lord commands the blessing at the place of unity

Psalm 133:1-3: "Behold, how good and how pleasant it is for brethren to dwell together in unity! It is like the precious ointment upon the head, that ran down upon the beard, even Aaron's beard: that went down to the skirts of his

*garments; As the dew of Hermon, and as the dew
that descended upon the mountains of Zion: for
there the Lord commanded the blessing, even life
for evermore."*

True zeal joins people together in united effort, in mind, in purpose and in sacrifices. Because it comes by the anointing of the Holy Spirit, it includes (as a person matures) the willingness to re-assess personal goals, desires and "needs" to see if they support the pursuit of the over-riding, shared goal.

Unity is compared to the holy anointing oil for preciousness (it is also shown to be an outcome of the Holy Spirit's anointing). WANT TO KNOW HOW ANOINTED YOU ARE? See if you are walking in unity with those around you.

Unity is also compared to the dew. In Palestine, the morning dew is what ensures the survival of all vegetation. Even crops depend heavily on dew. Dew alone can sustain a flourishing vineyard. In the hot desert, dew will fall only when no wind is stirring. By analogy, unity can happen only when all parties to a group maintain a peaceful, non-combative approach to solving problems and pursuing goals.

Ephesians 4:1-3, implies the "endeavoring to keep the unity of the Spirit in the bond of peace and will play a primary role in helping a believer walk worthy in the vocation wherewith ye are called."

Matthew 18:18-19, implies that the unity of two Christians in prayer moves God to act.

There seems to always be a constant battle when it comes to unifying two people or ideas to complete a whole. Have you ever wondered about this? It may be that unification is so powerful that it threatens your purpose or destiny. Knowing this, we strive for more unity in order to release God to move on our behalf.

Constant unity plays a primary role in releasing constant growth. In Acts 1:14, the believers were all with one accord in prayer just before the events of Pentecost, and they were in a single large meeting on the very day (Acts 2:1). They continued "with one accord" after Pentecost, and the Church grew daily, and was "having favor with all the people" in Jerusalem. Their unity reached the point of dissolving personal ownership of land, items and money into a corporate pool of resources (Acts 4:32).

Living in unity does not mean that we will agree on everything, there will be many opinions just as there are many notes in a musical chord. But we must agree on our purpose in life to work together for God. So just as the right notes on a piano combine together to make a beautiful sound, so should we agree to disagree in order to produce the right harmony with one another in our lives.

Unity: (1) makes the church a positive example to the world and helps draw others to us.

(2) Unity helps us cooperate as a body of believers as God means us to, giving us a foretaste of heaven.

(3) Unity renews and revitalizes ministry because there is less tension to sap our energy.

CHAPTER 8
HINDRANCES TO ACCESSING THIRD HEAVEN

Regarding Iniquity in the Heart

Psalm 66:17: *"I cried unto him with my mouth, and he was extolled with my tongue. If I regard iniquity in my heart, the Lord will not hear me; But verily God hath heard me; he hath attended to the voice of my prayer. Blessed be God, which hath not turned away my prayer, not his mercy from me."*

niquity is defined as the absence of moral or spiritual values, the powers of darkness, evil, and/or morally objectionable behavior. In essence, we cannot embrace Second Heaven activity hoping to reach into and obtain Third Heaven access. How can Beelzebub cast out Beelzebub? A Kingdom divided against itself cannot stand. Unforgiveness is iniquity in the heart that causes a stumbling block to a Third Heaven lifestyle. Is it worth your destiny to hold on to unforgiveness against someone or some situation that really no longer matters? Release yourself and your future from the iniquity in the heart.

Division

Since Christ launched the Church in the first century, evil forces emanating from Second Heaven have successfully caused many divisions among the believers in the Body of Christ. Many of these divisions later developed into split homes, communities, countries and divided churches. This has greatly hindered the cause of Christ to unbelievers. At the root of division is unforgiveness and pride. The right to be right oftentimes supersedes the need to express forgiveness. This division separates us as individuals from knowing the Will of God. When man's will overshadows God's Will, accessing Third Heaven becomes difficult if not impossible. The bible has much to say about unity and the blessings that are able to flow through that vain called unity.

Discouraging Other Believers

Through direct intervention and circumstances, some believers possess the ability to discourage other believers from accomplishing great things for God! This stems from doubting thoughts that may come from Second Heaven influences. As long as believers allow evil forces to place skeptical thoughts in their minds, which leads them into a state of leisure and laxness, a believer will never experience the joy and satisfaction that comes from the life of faith. There are times when you will have to walk this walk alone because of the negative influences that arise. You must determine that what you are leaving can't compare to what you are gaining! Know that you are never alone. God's Presence is always with you leading you into your Third Heaven purpose. Your Future is awaiting you.........so stay strong!

CHAPTER 9

THE GIFT OF A HANDICAP

"Because of the extravagance of those revelations, and so I wouldn't get a big head, I was given the gift of a handicap to keep me in constant touch with my limitations." [2 Corinthians 12:7 Message Bible]

Paul says he was given a "gift of a handicap" once he gained access to Third Heaven. This was given to him to keep him in constant touch with his limitations. Limitations are not always bad things. As a matter of fact, they can be viewed as safeguards. Without our limitations, we would become unbearable to others.

From the beginning of time, man has had limitations. The fruit of limitations is humility. In the Garden of Eden, Adam was given access to every tree. The one tree that he was not to eat from was the Tree of Knowledge of Good and Evil. This boundary or limitation was set in order for man to know that he is not God. After giving Adam everything that he needed, God's position was firmly established by creating this one boundary. Even within limitations, until you try them, you will never know where your boundaries lie. Some people live life so far beneath their boundaries and never really press beyond their pre-conceived limitations. To live a life and never seek to find the limitations is to have lived a life of regrets. Paul pressed beyond his natural limitations and experienced a place where he heard the unspeakable spoken and was forbidden to tell what he had heard. This press came from "forgetting his past failures and reaching toward the limitations in his life." In Philippians 3:13 Paul stresses: *"Don't get me wrong. By no means do I count myself an expert in all of this ....* (He is in touch with his limitations)*.... but I've got my eye on the goal. I'm off and running and I'm not turning back."* He was apparently moving forward, in spite of his own limitations. His goal was to get all that God had for him. His handicap was given to him because apparently what he heard was so fantastic that it would fail to keep him in touch with his own limitations. When we experience this magnitude of God's vision for us, at first glance it would cause us to think of ourselves more highly than we ought. Paul says that initially, he didn't consider this handicap a gift. But in fact, he said it "pushed him to his knees." Often times, handicaps are there for that very purpose, to keep us grounded. They are there for the purpose of bridging the gap between self-sufficiency and God sufficiency.

Handicaps are not always physical. They can be mental as well as emotional. Abuse, accidents, opposition, bad breaks, illnesses, insecurities, fear of failure, fear of rejection, age, family background, inferiority, unbelief, lack of education, physical and emotional limitations, etc. can all be viewed as *gifts of handicap*. While they may not be good by themselves, they will surely keep you anchored in your humanity. Some are very visible to others while the vast majority are invisible. That which is invisible is considered to exist in a dimension or realm. For instance, I believe Paul struggled with the fact that others did not accept him initially as an apostle. It may have given way to rejection in that realm.

I have often observed that people with the greatest handicaps often surpass others in achieving superior goals. They have learned to no longer operate from a First Heaven prospective, which is only temporal or physical, but they have looked past Second Heaven obstacles to consider them gifts with a purpose. They have viewed their success from a Third Heaven perspective, which is eternal. Paul says, "The weaker I get, the stronger I become." He had the right view of his handicaps. When we quit focusing on the handicap; begin appreciating them as gifts; and take our limitations in stride—-we begin to operate in a place where we realize that though we are weak, God's strength is what is ultimately moving us past our own limitations. We then understand that Third Heaven has no limitations.

QUESTIONS:

- Do you know what your limitations are?
- What are the things that have held you back from achieving your goals in life?
- What Third Heaven pursuits have you been afraid of?
- Why?

CHAPTER 10
OPENING A CLOSED HEAVEN

The Church is representative of the body of believers here on earth while the kingdom of the heaven is made up of both the earthly and heavenly realms. In order to effectively thrive in this First Heaven we must ensure that we know how to open a closed heaven and maintain passageway from us to God. Breakthrough is eminent when we discover the keys to opening a heaven that was once closed to us!

Malachi 3:10: "Bring all the tithes (the whole tenth of your income) into the storehouse, that there may be food in My house, and prove Me now by it, says the Lord of hosts, if I will not open the windows of HEAVEN for you and pour you out a blessing, that there shall not be room enough to receive it."

Giving

Giving opens the windows of heaven. This is a law that works like the law of gravity. No matter who does it, the principle works. It is a Third Heaven principle that works in opposition to the world's system. John 3:16 says *"For God so loved the world that he gave his only begotten son that whosoever believeth in him shall not perish, but they shall have everlasting life."*

God responds to your giving. He responded when Jesus gave His life. God will not allow you to out give Him. Luke 6:38 *"Give, and it will be given to you. A good measure, pressed down, shaken together and running over, will be poured into your lap. For with the measure you use, it will be measured to you."* Pouring usually denotes moving from one place to another in abundance. Giving allows the Third Heaven to now become open and revelation, provision, strategies, etc. will be poured out. You never come before a king without a gift. It's a principle given from heaven. Exodus 34:21 *"And none shall appear before Me empty-handed." [NKJV]*

According to Proverbs 18:16, *"A gift opens the way for the giver and ushers him into the presence of the great men."* To open the way indicates that the way must have at one point been closed. God the Father is a Giver. He gave the earth to man and said have dominion over it. When man forfeited that, He gave His Son, Jesus Christ. Jesus Christ gave Himself to save mankind from the consequences of sin. If we are going to pattern our lives after Christ, we are to be givers as well. The reason giving is so powerful is because it opens you up to God and tells Him that there is nothing that you would hold back from Him! When you give yourself fully and completely to God, it puts a demand on heaven to open up to you and release every promise that has been held up in the Second Heaven.

Obedience

Obedience is God's love language. He states simply "If you love Me, keep My commands." We honor God through our obedience to Him. When we obey Him, we are acknowledging that

He knows what is best for us. In the same way that our relationship with our children is strengthened when they obey our instruction, so it is with our heavenly father. Obedience gives us direct access to the Third Heaven. The bible says that Jesus was obedient, even unto the cross. This obedience yielded a great reward.

In 2 Chronicles 7:13 the Lord appeared before Solomon and said:

> *"If I shut up heaven that there be no rain, or if I command the locusts to devour the land, or if I send pestilence among my people; If my people which are called by my name shall humble themselves and pray and seek my face and turn from their wicked ways, then will I hear from heaven, and forgive their sin and heal their land."*

This scripture tells us how to open a closed heaven that has been shut up by God. (1) Humility, (2) prayer, (3) seeking the Face of God, and (4) repentance are the systems that will unlock Third Heaven.

Humility

Isaiah 57:15 "For thus says the high and lofty one – He Who inhabits eternity, Whose name is holy; I dwell in the high and holy place, but with him also who is of a thoroughly penitent and humble spirit, to revive the heart of the thoroughly penitent [bruised with sorrow for sin]." [Amplified Bible]

Our Heavenly Father is drawn to the humble. This scripture says he dwells with the humble. He inhabits eternity and those who are humble. Therefore, He brings Third Heaven to where we are when we humble ourselves. Some of His greatest promises are made to the humble.

As a result of placing more emphasis upon the role of the creature than the Creator, man exalts himself to a more lofty position and instills in himself the final authority of life. Man then becomes the god of his own life and destiny, ruling from a place called First Heaven. There is no wonder that humility is the avenue to Third Heaven breakthroughs.

Prayer

According to Acts10:9-11, Peter went up to the roof to pray his watch, about the sixth hour (noon), and fell into a trance. He saw the sky opened and something like a great sheet lowered and the four corners, descending to the earth. His prayer sent him into a trance and the heavens opened up in order for him to receive revelation from God. Prayer always opens up a closed heaven! When you need a Third Heaven answer to a First Heaven problem: just pray. Peter received a revelation from God, which changed the course of his life! We are able to do the same when we pray this prayer!

Dear Lord, I have come to a point in my journey with You that I feel like my life has become stagnant. Because I love You, I want to have more of Your Presence in my life. I know that if I gain access to Your Presence You will reveal to me the strategies for my next move. I declare and decree that the brass heavens are now open and Your revelation is pouring into me like never before. I humble myself before You, I seek Your face and I repent from doing things my way. I receive Your immeasurable love, joy, peace, strength, provision and strategies. In Jesus' Name. Amen!

Seeking God's Face

To seek God's Face is to come close to God in intimacy. It means to pursue His presence not merely His hand. His Hand is indicative of the things He does for us. To pass the hand and go directly to the face indicates the expressed love we have for God and His essence, His beauty, His greatness and most of all His Holiness. In a society where the focus is on acquiring the material things or First Heaven amenities in life, God in His Omniscience knows that this interrupts pure Third Heaven fellowship with Him. The heavens become closed because we stop reaching past what we are comfortable with in seeking the tangibles. God tells us to seek and we shall find. Half-hearted seeking however, devalues our relationship with God. Anything that we value, we go after whole-heartedly. Just as with any earthly relationship, there should be a longing for this type of intimacy. The lack of intimacy places distance between you and the one with whom you are in the relationship. Ultimately, the end result is lack of appreciation for what you have. We should be like the deer that pants for the water, longing after God!

Repentance

Repentance is merely turning around and going in the opposite direction. It is breaking a cycle in your life that has been leading nowhere. It is very important because without it, we would repeat the same cycles year in and year out without remorse or change. In order to move forward, you must STOP a negative behavior and START a positive one. Repentance is just that easy. It's not enough to be sorry for what we have done or not done, it is equally important to change direction, yielding control to our Heavenly Father who leads our lives from Third Heaven. The tendency is always for us to fall back into a comfortable, yet unproductive way of living our lives through Second Heaven responses. The challenge, my friend, is to resist the urge to get tuck in the old system (or way of thinking) in the natural or First Heaven realm.

CHAPTER II
MOVING WITH GOD

In order to understand how to navigate through the heavens, we have to have an understanding of such terms as: dimensions, realms, spheres, cycles, timing, systems, body, soul, spirit, and kingdom laws—- the language of the Kingdom. Understanding the language of a place causes you to operate more effectively in that environment.

A dimension is an extension in a given direction. Words like breadth, length, height and depth are dimensional terms. A dimension can't be touched physically, however a dimension can affect the physical and invisible realm. For instance, in the Gospel of Mark 4:35-41, the disciples were on a ship with Jesus in the midst of a great storm. Jesus rebuked the wind, and said unto the sea, "Peace, be still." At His direction, the wind ceased, and there was a great calm. The wind (dimensional) had an effect on the ship (physical). At that moment, Jesus was teaching the disciples that even though they are physical beings, their enacted faith could cause an atmospheric (physical) transformation. Whatever happens in one dimension affects every dimension. In plain terms, what we believe in our hearts can be manifested in our everyday lives.

Faith is also a dimensional term that can be extended in a given direction. The extension of the measure of faith is little faith. The extension of little faith is great faith. The "fruit of the Spirit" listed in Galatians 5:22-23 "love, joy, peace, long-suffering, gentleness, goodness, faith, meekness, temperance" is also dimensional. The fruit of the Spirit has the power to affect our bodies and surroundings, physically. For example, our environment and health are affected when there isn't any joy or peace. Although we can't physically touch joy or peace, that lack or presence of it can be seen. Jesus gives us an example of dimensional speaking. He rebuked the wind and it ceased and there was a great calm. As dimensional thinkers, we have power to call into existence peace, joy, love, etc. from another dimension. When we realize that we are more spiritual than physical, we will begin to live our lives as dimensional beings. In doing so, we will experience less defeat. However, we must have an understanding of the operation of the different dimensions in order to defeat or operate within each system.

We hear much talk of advancing to new levels. This type of thinking is typical of in-the-box thinkers, not dimensional thinkers. The thought process behind moving to a new level is that once I meet all the requirements of one level, I will be automatically qualified to move to the next level. This is a type of systematic thinking that uses man's systems in order to advance God's Kingdom. God's system is dimensional. Dimensional thinking, however, realizes that Jesus is the example. He didn't have limits or boundaries. He moved at a dimensional speed even though He was in a physical body.

Now what is often missed in reading Genesis is that in addition to the physical, material world, God also created an invisible SPIRITUAL realm. In the New Testament this is called "the heavenlies" or "the heavenly places." The spiritual realm is a created part of the universe, which has different characteristics and obeys different laws than the physical world. For example, in the physical world we have the law of gravity. Simply stated, what goes up must come down. In the spiritual world there exists the law of dimensions. Eternity, for example, doesn't have a beginning or an end, nor an up or down. However, when one accepts Jesus Christ as his Lord and Savior, he immediately has eternal life. God doesn't have a beginning or end. He is higher than the highest, lower than the lowest and deeper than the deepest. He brought forth out of nothing the material world in the creation story.

Man is a creature who was made to live simultaneously in both realms. We were created to operate in the physical and spiritual realm because we are both physical and spiritual beings. If we are to live successful and effective lives, we must learn the systems of all three heavens.

In the book of Revelation, notice how the scene switches back and forth from earth to heaven. Then as the book unfolds, the heavens open up (are "revealed" or unveiled) and things now hidden from plain view in the material world are made known. That is, the world of the invisible breaks in upon us. At the beginning of Chapter 4 of Revelation, the scene switches from earth to heaven. John is invited to step outside the physical world through a door into the eternal, spiritual realm. John was in the Spirit on the Lord's Day. He is able to move from earth (First Heaven) to Third Heaven, effectively. Revelation 4 is outside our space-time domain but these are real events, which he describes. What John sees going on in the Throne Room of the Universe affects events in history that have unfolded, are unfolding and will unfold shortly. Now he can effectively write to the churches about where they are presently in the timetable of history. Time has different properties in heaven, so events in heaven are not locked in step with the time flow of world history.

GOD'S TIMING

I Chronicles 12:32 states *"And of the children of Issachar, which were men that had understanding of the times, to know what Israel ought to do; the heads of them were two hundred; and all their brethren were at their commandment."*

The Scripture tells us clearly that God has a calendar for planet earth. There are times and seasons in His purpose for the heavens and the earth. His timing is not the same as ours. For that reason we must learn to discern the times. We must especially be aware of God's timetable; like the men of the ancient tribe of Issachar, who understood the times and knew what Israel should do. We need divine insight into Third Heaven to discern the purposes for our generation. We must also understand where we are headed as we approach the end of the Church age.

This isn't to say that we can know the exact date of Jesus' return. The Lord told His disciples: *"No one knows the day or hour, not even the angels in heaven, nor the Son, but only the Father"* (Matthew 24:36). Paul added this warning when he told the Thessalonians: *"Now brothers, about times and dates, we do not need to write you, for you know very well that the day of the Lord will come like a thief in the night"* (I Thessalonians 5:1, 2).

GOD'S MOVEMENT

God seems to do something different with His people approximately every 2,000 years (a dimension), every 500 years (a realm), every 50 years (a sphere) and every 10 years (a cycle). If you allow for a variance of 10-40 years in either side of some rounded dates you will begin to see an emerging pattern.

For example in the year 0 God made the human race when He made Adam (Genesis 1:26-28). Moses wrote about this in the Pentateuch. Moses had been able to see into a dimension that was not yet in natural existence. He was therefore able to write about eternal events that had happened in Third Heaven. Isaiah was also able to see in this dimension of heaven (Isaiah 6:1-8) when king Uzziah died. He saw the Lord sitting upon a throne, high and lifted up, and His train filled the temple. He saw seraphim and he heard the Voice of the Lord speaking with the Trinity.....vs. 8 "Also I heard the voice of the Lord, saying, Whom shall I send, and who will go for us? Then said I, Here am I; send me." Isaiah was also able to see into and write from a Third Heaven position. This allowed him to position himself for the next move of God.

Approximately two thousand years later, God called Abraham to found the Hebrew nation (Genesis 17:1-8). He positioned himself to move with God. John the Baptist came before the Lord in the spirit and power of Elijah ...to make ready a people prepared for the Lord. He was a single prophet who prepared for the personal coming of Jesus Christ. He heralds the end of an old dimension (approximately 2000 years) and the beginning of a new one....the Church Age. No doubt Third Heaven activity was one of excitement when John began to come forth because it meant Jesus' time was at hand. John's ministry released the time for Jesus to be activated and manifested as the Messiah. He moved with God.

Jesus Christ established the Church upon Peter's Third Heaven revelation of Jesus Christ. Matthew 6:16-19. The keys of the kingdom of the heavens (access) are now given to him. A more accurate translation of verse nineteen from the Greek is, *"And I will give thee the keys of the kingdom of the heavens. And whatever thou shalt bind on the earth shall be as having been bound in the heavens; and whatever thou shalt loose on the earth shall be as having been loosed in the heavens."* Before these verses can be correctly understood, a distinction must be made between the Church and the kingdom of the heavens. The Church is representative of the body of believers here on earth while the kingdom of the heavens is made up of both the earthly and heavenly realms.

Now yet another 2000 years later God is moving and the Church age is soon to become the Kingdom Age – a dimension with immortal bodies and immortal spirits. At that time we will receive renewed, glorified bodies to serve the Kingdom of God. With that same excitement, there is momentum in Third Heaven as Jesus prepares for His Second Coming ushering in a new dimension! You and I are being activated for this very purpose…to move with God. We must discern the times emanating from Third Heaven, so that our purpose will be fulfilled.

So as you can see, we are in the end of the 6,000th year from the creation of Adam or the 6th day. 2 Peter 3:8-9 states *"But do not forget this one thing, dear friends: With the Lord a day is like a thousand years, and a thousand years are like a day. The Lord is not slow in keeping his promise, as some understand slowness. Instead he is patient with you, not wanting anyone to perish, but everyone to come to repentance."* The present dimension is about to shift from Church Age to Kingdom which means at the end of this sixth day period, God's government is going to be restored to its rightful place. When this happens, we will walk in the fullness of the restoration of immeasurable blessings! Are you ready to move with God?

Within each dimension is a realm of approximately 500-year increments of God's calendar movement. When man fell, God's government was destroyed and deterioration set in. Once chaos began to be the order of the day, the enemy had legal access to the Body of Christ. Then repentance came and after repentance restoration. For centuries, this was the cycle of life here in First Heaven. Five centuries after Jesus established the Church, it was still going through these cycles of deterioration, repentance and restoration. Approximately another five hundred years later, A.D. 1000 was the mid-night of those Dark Ages. Soon after the years A.D. 1500 the great restoration of the Church began. I believe that in the not too distant future we will see the restoration of the Church completed. God has already begun it! The bible says that Jesus is being held in the heavens (Third Heaven) until the time of the restoration of all things (Acts 3:21). When this restoration is finally complete, we will see the return of Jesus!

Within each realm is a sphere or approximately 50-year increments, which represent generations that are born. This is where we begin to see generational blessings and curses develop. The bible is clear on this in 2 Chronicles where we see kings reigning, either leading Israel or Judah in worship of God or idolatry, then dying and their sons reigning and carrying on the curses or reversing the curses of the previous generations.

Just as today, if we examine our present day generations, we can trace blessings or curses that transfer from generation to generation.

Within each sphere is an approximately 10 year increment or season. This is called a cycle. Genesis 8:22 and Ecclesiastes 3:1-8 give the indication that as long as there is a dimension called Third Heaven we will experience ongoing cycles or patterns of life experiences in First Heaven. This cycle of life is: (1) Rest, (2) Rebellion, (3) Retribution (4) Repentance and (5) Restoration. Once this cycle is complete, it repeats itself.

Activity in Third Heaven, warfare in Second Heaven and manifestation in the First Heaven accompany each major move of God. First of all, John's prophetic ministry released the time for Jesus to be activated and manifested as the Messiah, with mighty demonstrations of the Holy Spirit's power. John was a sign that the dimension of Law was ending and the dimension of Grace was emerging. Undoubtedly, all heaven got excited and began to celebrate when John began to come forth as a prophet and his ministry was manifested. This meant that Jesus' time was at hand. When Jesus was born, the angels came from Third Heaven to First Heaven rejoicing and praising God. When the Apostle John was given a look into Third Heaven (the future), he recorded that he saw sevens angels with trumpets. Each time one of those angels in Third Heaven blew a trumpet, something happened on earth (First Heaven). Today, Jesus is the one who is celebrating our access to this dimension called Third Heaven. We have been activated and given access to accomplish our purpose here in the earth. Whatever is loosed in Third Heaven by the angels is also loosed in First Heaven by us who have access to Third Heaven. In other words, what is decreed and released in heaven is decreed and released here on earth. We should be aware that until it is decreed in heaven and the trumpet is sounded, it won't manifest. Therefore, we must be like the sons of Issachar and discern the times. We are at the 6,000-year mark, the 6th day and the angels are positioning themselves to sound the trumpet for the return of Jesus. Third Heaven people will sense uneasiness in their Spirits that they may not be able to pinpoint exactly. You may be feeling the activity in Third Heaven!

MAN'S MOVEMENT AND GOD'S TIMING

Timing is determined within cycles, spheres, realms and dimensions. Each has its own timing. Knowing when to move at the correct time within a cycle, sphere, realm or dimension will determine whether or not you find yourself walking in your correct place of purpose with God.

The ancient Greeks had two words for time: chronos and kairos. In the New Testament kairos means "the appointed time in the purpose of God or the time when God acts." It is a moment of undetermined period of time in which something special happens. Doing good to all people is a First Heaven act, which will inevitably produce Third Heaven fruit of reaping a harvest. The timing, however, is God's timing that will be fulfilled at the proper time in your life. This particular timing is the right or perfect time. Man cannot control it, however man must be open and trusting enough to move in God's timing.

We tend to think of our time within a chronos or chronological sequential mindset (First Heaven), which is measured by a clock or calendar. We think of life in terms of 24-hour days, seven-day weeks, and 52-week years. We define our lives this way. This kind of mindset is very limiting and doesn't allow for the limitless moves of God in our lives. We must remember that God operates from Third Heaven or a kairos place. He is not limited by time. He may be trying to do something at an accelerated pace in your life! It is our job to discern and have an understanding of the right time in order to know what God is doing. We have got to change from a chronos to a kairos mindset. As we move with God, we will know what to do at just the right time. There are others waiting for you to discern God's timing in your life! As you move in God's timing, those attached to you move in His timing as well.

Procrastination is an enemy to man's ability to move in God's timing. It is the act of putting off or delaying something requiring immediate attention. It reflects our struggle with being in control since we are unable to accurately predict how things will turn out. The reason why it's specifically an enemy to kairos timing is because we have to yield to the power of the God of an invisible world, and rely on a positive result to manifest in the visible world.

All the events of history have been fit into God's timetable. God's purpose has been carried out specifically in regard to your life. The only way to find true happiness while operating in kairos time is in knowing that in God's providence, all events will be worked out for your good!

Note that timing has to do with the purpose of a thing. If we discern the times, we won't throw stones in a time we should be gathering them. We won't pluck up seeds when we should be planting them. This system goes against the chronos to produce a kairos moment in our lives. There are times when we sense in our spirits that we should be moving against what would seem like the natural thing to do at a particular time. When we move with what we sense God is saying, we then begin to bring about a Third Heaven purpose for our lives. Most of the time, moving like this is uncomfortable, but it is a necessity when bringing into manifestation God's promises to us!

In order to understand how a thing works, you must first understand the system within which it is working. In other words, we must have an understanding of cause and effect. When God formed man in Genesis 2:7, he was formed with every system already inside of him that man needed for successful operation. The digestive system, respiratory system, nervous system, circulatory system, excretory system, etc. Each system is interdependent upon one another. It wasn't until God breathed into man that those systems came to life and became functional. In our spiritual lives, God has created this same invisible system. This system is in opposition to the world's system of thinking of which Satan is the author. And Satan encourages people to develop mistaken beliefs about the goals they need to reach to achieve true happiness.

However, you are seated in a position of authority and dominion. Ephesians 2:6 says that *"He hath raised us up together, and made us sit together in heavenly places in Christ Jesus."* This is our Third Heaven position. Ephesians 1:21 tells us where these heavenly places are: *"Far above all principality, and power, and might, and dominion, and every name that is named, not only in this world, but also in that which is to come."*

All that you are struggling with is underneath you. Every invisible system that has been designed by the enemy to stop you has to cease! You have authority over it. From your seated position in Christ Jesus, every plan and implementation that is in opposition to God's order has no authority to operate in your life! It's illegal and must be arrested. God has given dominion to you over it! Your Third Heaven perspective gives you authority over your life. Be free. Command your life from your Third Heaven position!

CONCLUSION

ow that we have discovered that paradise was lost, and how we can regain it (in the First, Second and Third Heavens), there aren't any excuses holding us back from the greatest seasons of our lives. We are now ready to manifest the Kingdom of God.

The charge to the reader is to know and discern the movement of God in your life. There is momentum in the heavenlies that is signaling to you that God is doing something fantastic in your life. He wants us to be ready to move with Him. He wants us to be in position for favor like never before! He wants us to walk step by step with Him to accomplish the wonderful plans He has for us.

The world is waiting to see the manifestation of God through you. Yes, you who are reading this book! Don't die with your purpose unfulfilled. Squeeze out everything that God has placed inside of you. Write that book! Start that business! Be the catalyst for change in the government! Teach the next generation! Go back to school and finish that education! Start that ministry! Light the fire under your feet! There is spiritual activity all around you signaling that it's your time for forward movement. Third Heaven is bustling with excitement awaiting your next move. Are you ready? There is greater for you! Greater is available to you now. Many of us have yearned and desired to have more in the way of fulfillment in this life. Sometimes, we have journeyed year in and year out only to come to a place wondering, 'Lord is this it, or is there more to life than this?' The good news is that the victorious, abundant and satisfying life is available to you right here, right now on earth through accessing Third Heaven! What was lost can now be regained. You are never too young or too old to experience bringing heaven to earth! THE TIME IS NOW TO ACCESS THIRD HEAVEN!

ABOUT THE AUTHOR

*W*ANDA J. SISCO, M.Div., D.Min. is the Overseer and Founder of Beyond the Veil Worship Center with locations in Upper Marlboro, Maryland and Northeast Washington, DC. She is also the founder of International Kingdom Women's Coalition, an organization that supports the vision of female Kingdom Leaders and helps them achieve their purpose in life. She is the President of Next Dimension Global Alliance, LLC. providing networking opportunities, leadership training and mentoring to Ecclesiastical and Marketplace Leaders. As a Professional Certified Life Coach, her coaching practice *Journey to Wholeness, LLC*. empowers people to meet their various life, relationship and professional goals.

Dr. Sisco frequently ministers in various conferences, workshops and retreats with a Third Heaven message that reaches the masses. She has been blessed to spread the Gospel of Jesus Christ throughout the United States and many foreign countries. For more information, visit the website at beyondtheveilministries.org or contact her at pastorsisco@beyondtheveilministries.org.

CPSIA information can be obtained
at www.ICGtesting.com
Printed in the USA
FSOW03n1512280916
25505FS

9 781498 446389